"This is a brilliant book."

—JOHN KRETSCHMER

Author *Sailing a Serious Ocean* and *At the Mercy of the Sea*

"Sailing, like all sport in its purest form, is meant to be a metaphor for life. Through *Sea Trials* Peter Bourke takes us on an adventure, not only singlehanded across the North Atlantic, but more importantly on a journey through one man's life. The elegantly crafted and artfully worded story offers us a view into the triumphs, difficulties, and foibles Bourke has faced, and through those anecdotes we see shadows of ourselves and some of the issues we've faced in our own experiences. Sailing is the vehicle upon which the larger cargo of life is conveyed. Page by page, *Sea Trials* is truly a treasure."

—BILL BIEWENGA

SEA TRIALS

SEA TRIALS

A LONE SAILOR'S RACE TOWARD HOME

PETER J. BOURKE

International Marine / McGraw-Hill Education
Camden, Maine | New York | Chicago | San Francisco
Lisbon | London | Madrid | Mexico City | Milan | New Delhi
San Juan | Seoul | Singapore | Sydney | Toronto

1 2 3 4 5 6 7 8 9 10 11 12 13 14 15 QFR/QFR 1 9 8 7 6 5 4
ISBN 978-0-07-182192-6
MHID 0-07-182192-9
E ISBN (color) 0-07-182196-1

Library of Congress Cataloging-in-Publication Data is available from the Library of Congress.

McGraw-Hill Education books are available at special quantity discounts to use as premiums and sales promotions or for use in corporate training programs. To contact a representative, please e-mail us at bulksales@mcgraw-hill.com.

Questions regarding the content of this book should be addressed to www.internationalmarine.com

Questions regarding the ordering of this book should be addressed to
McGraw-Hill Education
Customer Service Department
P.O. Box 547
Blacklick, OH 43004
Retail customers: 1-800-262-4729
Bookstores: 1-800-722-4726

Photos pages viii, 16, 34, and 156 courtesy John Jamieson.

For Amy and Steven

CONTENTS

INTRODUCTION

Bill, with whom I've just crossed the Atlantic, secures his seabag and turns to me. "Remember," he says, "all you need to finish the race are a hull and a sail." He knows that equipment problems will play a role in the event, as they always do in ocean races, and he's using his last minutes before heading to the airport to remind me that some perseverance may well be required. Mike, our third crewmember on the just-completed passage, is already ashore exploring Plymouth before catching a train to London.

The race in question is the 2009 OSTAR (Original Single-handed Trans-Atlantic Race), which goes back to 1960. It's a romp across the North Atlantic, with the start in Plymouth Sound on the southwest coast of England and the finish in Narragansett Bay, just outside Newport Harbor on the coast of Rhode Island. The starting gun is scheduled to fire in seven days.

It is exciting to be here, but I can't help feeling that I'm an imposter in a major-league lineup who's about to be found out. Unfortunately, there is a factual basis for this view as I've been sailing for only about ten years, and many of those had little sailing in them. Two years after losing Gail, my wife of seventeen years, I enrolled in a learn-to-sail course. Six months later I bought my first boat, a lightly used and lovely sloop with the wonderful name *Steadfast*. A few years later I said goodbye to *Steadfast* and bought *Rubicon*, a strong, fast, and beautiful sea boat.

I have a sense now of what I was searching for when I took up sailing, but at the time I simply knew that I needed a boat, only dimly aware that I was on a voyage of exploration, a quest for an open passage to the other side of loss. But it was OK because I justified the purchase as the perfect vacation home to enjoy with my young children. The boat was indeed that, before it became the portal to an earlier dream of ocean passagemaking. I embraced the evolution, believing that such sailing would clear my mind, rejuvenate my spirit, and allow me to be a better parent. That was my story then, and I've always stuck to it.

Those events are now a decade ago and an ocean away. *Rubicon*, my Outbound 44, lies sparkling in the bright light of morning, looking refreshed from her transatlantic passage. She is secured to the dock in front of the Royal Western Yacht Club in Plymouth, England, a five-minute walk from the old stone steps trod by the pilgrims as they embarked on a new life in a new world. Beyond the many boats clustered in the marina rests the broad expanse of Plymouth Harbor, said to be the finest harbor in western Europe. It is the harbor where Drake's fleet sailed with the tide for its rendezvous with the Spanish Armada, and the harbor where American and British troopships weighed anchor and pointed their bows toward Normandy. Arriving at first light, I felt the sense of history that is a part of the atmosphere in places where world events have turned. It's just a sailboat race, but I am conscious of being the only American on this year's roster. Thirty-one sailors are scheduled to make the start, in boats ranging from a fast 50-foot trimaran to strong cruising boats such as *Rubicon*, all theoretically equalized by their various ratings. Though the racers are predominantly British, the flags of many countries will be flying at the start. The stars and stripes are already flying at their station on *Rubicon's* transom.

Before taking his leave, Bill adds, "At the end of the day, the OSTAR, or any solo transatlantic, is not about the sailing." I smile, as his comment strikes a harmonic note in my mind, even as my left brain is whispering, "Say what?" However, there is only time to nod sagely before Bill wishes me luck, we have our handshakes, and I am alone on the boat. I have a week to make ready for the return voyage and, as it will turn out, many long days to consider Bill's comment as I fight my way back to Newport. Of course it's about the sailing. How can you cross an ocean by yourself, let alone be competitive in a race, if you don't focus on the sailing? Out there, staying alive is all about the sailing. Being alive, of course, is about a great many things.

DAY 1
LOSS

Adversity introduces a man to himself.
—SENECA

etting to the start line is half the battle—a truism in sailboat racing as in life. Well, I'm crossing that start line now, gliding past in a mere 7 knots of breeze, but we are over it and the second half of the battle begins. "Thank God for these conditions," I mutter. Racing starts can be dicey affairs as fast boats and large egos converge. A few seconds more or less in a weeks-long race is not worth a collision, and the boats look more like they are passing in review than starting a race, except for the trimaran, which has embraced these light winds and skittered away like a butterfly. *Rubicon* and I are bound for Newport, just shy of three thousand nautical miles to the west-southwest of Plymouth, England. Time enough to think of many things, but for now I'm concentrating on the traffic: competitors, press boats, and spectator boats, not to mention the good ship *Galatea*, where His Royal Highness Prince Philip has just signaled the start. From here he just looks like a big fellow in a dark coat.

The breeze is light but steady and it is keeping the boats moving and cleanly separated as they cross the start, that imaginary line in the water between the race committee boat, in this case the *Galatea*, and Melampus buoy. Once over the line, I relax for a moment and enjoy the spectacle. There's pageantry to the whole affair, with spectators waving and the prince in attendance, and of

Rubicon sailing in Plymouth, England, before the start of the 2009 OSTAR.

course no one does pageantry better than the Brits. It seems we will clear Eddystone Light without the need to tack. Tacking is the generally simple process of steering the bow of the boat through the wind, and adjusting the sails as the wind begins to drive them from the new side. There are only two tacks in sailing: port when the wind is coming over the left side of the boat, and starboard when the breeze hits the right side of the boat first. You tack when the wind's direction suggests that a better line to the goal, to the next waypoint in your journey, is more obtainable by "taking a different tack."

The racing instructions for the OSTAR are short and simple: they require that you leave the Eddystone Lighthouse on your starboard side and—a few thousand miles later—that you also leave Nantucket Island to starboard. These are sensible instructions that reduce the risk that you will lose your boat to the rocks on either side of the Atlantic. The middle part is up to you.

The wind builds steadily through the afternoon, from the mild start up into the teens, and it's now hitting 16 knots. A knot is a nautical mile, which is slightly longer than our road miles—1.15 times to be exact—so 16 knots is approximately an 18-mile-per-hour wind, a fantastic breeze for sailing, and *Rubicon* is humming along. The thirty-one boats that made the start are separating as the faster ones stretch their legs. As the afternoon light fades, I can still see half a dozen boats, with two about a mile ahead and the rest close behind. It is pleasant to be sailing with this band of enthusiasts, amateurs all, but I know that by tomorrow morning it is unlikely that any of us will be within sight of each other. It's a big ocean, and we each have our own ideas on the best line to the finish. The only thing that's certain is that it won't be a straight line.

Despite having the chart taped to the table down below, it has been hard for me to dislodge my mental picture of the English Channel as similar to the lower Hudson River as it borders Manhattan, a beehive of activity with boats and ships of all shapes and sizes. The idea of sailing down the channel alone has been a more intimidating prospect than any particular stretch of the North Atlantic that may lie ahead. My perspective was broadened a week ago when we arrived, though dawn was just breaking as we entered Plymouth Sound and focused on finding our way safely past the breakwater outside the harbor. This is not the Hudson River, or the Thames. It is the bloody English Channel, a sea by all appearances. It is a wide stretch of water and it has kept the continental hounds at bay for centuries.

It is no doubt foolish to think too far ahead, but *Rubicon* is flying now and if we can keep up the pace we should be able to finish at least with the main pack. I completed a transatlantic only a week ago, yet my appetite for sailing seems as ravenous as ever, and this afternoon is exhilarating. There are no commercial ships in sight, and it feels as if the channel—one of the busiest waterways in the world—has been cleared for our private race.

The race is 8 hours old and we are already passing the Lizard, the southernmost point of land on the island of Britain. The Lizard

Light went on line in 1751, the lighthouse being one of the more powerful forms of communication in its day, and its welcome glow is clearly visible. For many years it has defined the end point for transatlantic speed records. It is comforting to see its light, giving warning of where not to go.

The next objective is to clear the Scilly Isles. The Scillies are an archipelago of 145 islands, or at least outcroppings, though the population of about two thousand people has spread out to only five of them. They are sprinkled about 30 miles southwest of the mainland. I will want to leave Bishop Rock and its 45-meter lighthouse on my starboard side. According to the *Guinness World Records*, Bishop Rock is the smallest island in the world with a building on it. I'm more interested in the fact that it marks the westernmost point of the archipelago, and the UK, and I can then relax a bit knowing there is nothing but open ocean ahead.

As the light fades I decide on chicken in black bean sauce, one of the dozen prepared dinners I picked up in Sainsbury's grocery, and I turn on the small propane oven in the galley. The enjoyment of food is always amplified on a boat—perhaps it's the "camping effect"—and tonight's repast is no exception.

The rush of the race down the English Channel has worn off, and a wave of fatigue washes over me, probably as much from the frenetic pace of the past week as from today's exertions, but I cannot yet succumb to the temptations of sleep. *Rubicon* is equipped with an AIS (Automatic Identification System), which will sound an alarm if a ship comes within 10 miles, but I've switched off the alarm as one ship after another converges on the mouth of the channel. Heavy clouds are blanketing the sky, and the only light piercing the inky blackness comes from the twinkling navigation lights of the OSTAR boats and the large ships as they pass.

The wind has stiffened and it's blowing about 25 knots, so I throw a reef in the mainsail to reduce the sail area stretched from the mast. Offshore sailing is a 24/7 enterprise. There is nowhere to anchor, so as long as there's wind, the boat will keep powering forward. However, a boat can take only so much wind in her sails without becoming overpowered. The prudent mariner, as well as the most competitive racer, will spend considerable time tucking in reefs and shaking them back out as conditions change during a passage. Putting a reef in the mainsail is an efficient way of depowering a boat and, with the autopilot steering, it's usually a simple matter to lower the sail sufficiently for the reef hook to be secured.

With all secure on deck, I go below and settle in at the navigation station, or nav desk, conveniently located close to the galley. The nav desk is my office on the boat, where the computer glows and all of the boat's instruments can be monitored. The nav desk is perhaps the one area on a modern sailboat where the functions would not be quickly apparent to a mariner from the earliest days of sail. From the nav desk you can monitor, control, and communicate. Here I am surrounded by instruments and switches, yet somehow it feels cozy. It's the wood, of course, a dark, rich African cherry. Topside is all fiberglass, stainless steel, and aluminum; thank God nothing to varnish. Down below, I am reminded of a manor home, albeit a very small one. The total square footage of *Rubicon's* living space would not equal that of the smallest studio apartment, yet it is warm and welcoming. I can also eat at my desk here, just as I used to do in the office, and I sometimes sleep here (which was not one of my regular work habits). It is even possible to effect a minor change in course without going on deck by making small adjustments to the autopilot's control unit. As always, significant course changes require some effort and adjustments to the sails.

It has been a long day already and I know there will be little sleep till we are over the continental shelf and in deeper water, but I allow myself a short nap. Today may go down as one of my best days, but my thoughts return to the worst.

The call came just after four o'clock on a Tuesday afternoon in early September 1996. Stacy, a young assistant in our young firm, stuck her head in my office and announced, "Your father-in-law is on the line. He says it's urgent." Of course I would have taken Ray's call without his message of urgency, but that was my first intimation that it would be a very ugly day. It was a short conversation.

Ray: "It's Gail, I think we've lost her."
Me: (After a pause) "Seizure?"

Ray:	"Yes."
Me:	(Swallowing hard) "Is she dead?"
Ray:	"I think it's already too late."
Me:	"I'm on my way."

I raced out of the office, ran down the two floors to the parking garage, jumped behind the wheel, and drove like I'd never driven before. I understood Ray's words—his mind knew that he had lost a daughter, but his heart could not yet accept that fact. Both my heart and my mind received it the same way. I'm sure I knew that I had lost my wife, but I clung to a spark of hope that Ray had been mistaken, and Gail was even now recovering in the hospital. Few had cell phones in 1996, and I had not yet felt the requirement, so I would have no further information for the next hour as I hurtled my Honda down the Garden State Parkway, crying, praying, and steering. Amazingly, I escaped the notice of the police cruisers who fish for speeders on the state's main artery. I had not prayed so hard in many years, in all my life really, but as I turned the corner onto my block I knew that my prayers had failed. I had lost my wife. In front of my house were half a dozen cars and standing on the lawn were two of my neighbors. They were both crying. I parked drunkenly at the curb. Before I could say anything, Louise, our neighbor from across the street, came up to me and, in a soft voice colored in sorrow, she said, "I'm so sorry." I asked her if she was sure and when she said yes, I leaned over the roof of my car and wept.

As I steeled myself to walk through the front door, I noted the different cars and whom to expect. There was Gail's parents' Honda, behind it the Volvo of her sister and her husband, and at the curb were a couple of cars I did not recognize. More cars and stunned friends and family would arrive before nightfall. As I walked in the house and exchanged tearful embraces I saw that Dr. Fuhrman, a longtime friend of Gail's family, was also there.

Dr. Fuhrman told me that the paramedics and the police had already come and gone, but they had held off on calling the funeral home to allow me a chance to say goodbye. I went upstairs and found Gail lying lifeless in our bed. I felt like I'd been punched in the chest, hard. Only forty-two, she was the touchstone of my life and the lives of our children and her extended family. She had lunched with her sister just hours before, but apparently felt under the weather and returned home to lie down till it was time to pick up the children from school. Gail died in our bed from a seizure. When we were first engaged, Gail told me about her seizure disorder. She had been the target of this affliction since she was a teenager, and I guess she thought that full disclosure was important. Neither of us expected it to be lethal. I saw what had hit me, but I could hardly absorb it then. I simply needed to soldier on. After a time, I bent over for a last kiss and the outline of the pledge formed in my mind. Of course it was for Amy and Steven, our eight- and ten-year-old children, and I would make it many times in the years ahead. I whispered the words and kissed her goodbye.

The most terrible day of my life was playing out, but the true terror lay ahead. I would have to tell the children. We lived in a close-knit neighborhood in Westfield, as lovely a town as New Jersey has to offer, and a town where mothers, and the occasional father, came out to escort the children walking the two blocks from the elementary school. A neighbor had walked the children home from the school, but they were unable to go inside as their mother had died inside our locked home. The children were taken to friends' homes, both on the same block, a minute's walk apart. Steven was playing with his buddy Richie, and Amy with her friend Claire. As yet they knew nothing of their loss. Gail's parents lived only a mile away, and as Gail had kept her maiden name when we got married in 1979, a practice then growing in acceptance, their number was quickly found. So it was that her parents faced that nightmare of all parents, without warning or preparation, and found the courage that the day required.

Before I undertook these deeds, the first of the long parade of sad arrangements needed attention. Dr. Fuhrman said we needed to call the funeral home, and that it should be done before I went to get the children. In what I imagine was some gesture of acknowledgment that I was the husband, he placed the call and handed me the phone. I held the receiver for a few moments but could not bring any words out. Dr. Fuhrman gently took the phone from my hands and made the arrangements. I then went into the living room where I listened as the minister, who had arrived while

I was upstairs, read the Twenty-Third Psalm. Finding my voice, I asked him to repeat it, knowing I would need every ounce of strength it could give me. Someone made tea.

The people from the funeral home did their duty, and did so with efficiency and kindness, and I found the strength to walk out the door and around to the other side of the block to get Steven. After standing on the doorstep for a few minutes I took a deep breath and knocked. The parents knew, and said whatever one could say under the circumstances, though I no longer recall their words. After a brief conversation with them I took Steven outside. I sat him down on the porch, looked him in the eyes, and told him that I had some terrible news that I had to tell him. I then told him that his mother had died. His beaming face simply crumbled, tears erupted, and then he wailed, "It's not fair." Truer words were never spoken. After providing what comfort I could, I walked him home to the arms of his grandparents. Without pausing, I turned around to do it again. I went to the home where Amy was still playing. The scenario unfolded the same way as with Steven, except that Amy's smiling and lovely face did not crumble. Her beautiful dark complexion reflected anguish, and a certain fierceness, and then she started to sob. It was a very angry sadness and tears were flowing. My heart was again pierced when on our short walk home, and no more than 15 minutes after hearing this devastating news, she said, with as profound a sadness as I ever want to hear, "Daddy, I've lost two mothers now." It was a reference to the fact that she was adopted. We adopted both our children from Chile as infants. They knew they had lost their birth mothers. Now they would have to adjust to life without any mother.

If it had been just the grief, I might have let myself go. If it had been only the new responsibilities, I might have shaken with fear, but the twin realities pulled at each other, creating a tension that left me wobbly but standing. And so it was for a while.

Lizard Light has fallen below the horizon behind us as we drive through the night. I send a couple of e-mails to friends saying that *Rubicon* is doing 8 knots in 14 knots of breeze and heading west. I can't ask for more.

FREEDOM

If I am not for myself, who will be?
If I am only for myself, who am I?
If not now, when?

—TALMUD

The ship's clock reads a few minutes after 0300 and there is splashing inside the boat. A cardinal rule of sailing is to keep the sea on the other side of the hull, so this can't be a good thing. Sleep dissolves and the investigation is brief. We're cleaving a straight path, but the meeting of bow and waves has water cascading over the foredeck, washing its way down the flanks of the boat and, I discover, splashing in through one of the windows, or hatches, in the main cabin. Any opening in the deck of a boat can be referred to as a hatch, which is why we "batten down the hatches" when rough weather is anticipated. This one was obviously opened in Plymouth and then not fully dogged down, and I have only myself to blame for that little bit of stupidity. A few wet cushions are a small price to pay for a problem resolved.

Rubicon's attitude as she leans into the oncoming waves announces that it's time to reduce sail area, to take in another reef. It is always easier to shake out a reef than to put one in, so I lower the big mainsail to the third and last reef point. We are sailing close-hauled (pointing close to the wind), so what sailors call the apparent wind—the real wind hitting the sails—is stronger than the true wind. It's like walking into the wind versus walking with the wind at your back. But even the true wind is now pushing 30 knots and gusting higher, approaching Force 7 territory by Admiral Beaufort's scale and a fair bit of breeze. The passage from Newport reminded me many times that *Rubicon* would not lose speed as I reefed her sails in a building wind. She would simply settle down for a smoother ride.

One of my stay-alive disciplines is to never leave the cockpit without wearing my harness and whispering a command to be careful. Tonight is definitely a clip-on night, and the click of the closing shackle is comforting. On *Rubicon* most of the control lines lead back to the cockpit, but every reef taken in or let out requires a quick trip forward to secure or release the reefing hook at the mast. The small LED light on my headband provides working light, and it is short work to secure the reef in the mainsail.

Free-falling from the deck, plunging into the cold and dark waters, and spluttering to the surface in time to watch your boat sail away and over the horizon is the purest form of terror for a solo sailor. You will never catch the boat. I am terrified of such an end, or rather I would be if I allowed my mind to dwell on it. The mistake of falling overboard would certainly be the last one I would make in this life. It is a death sentence, pure and simple. If you happened to have one of the small EPIRBs (emergency position-indicating radio beacons) attached to your flotation jacket, you could hope for rescue before hypothermia and death set in, but you would only entertain that hope because its hollow promise was all you had left. The answer is simple—stay on the damn boat. Wear a harness with a couple of tethers so you can attach the second before you release the first as you move about the boat, watch for waves, stay vigilant, and then close the box on that particular fear.

The sail plan is now a triple-reefed main and the one reef in the solent headsail, leaving *Rubicon* with plenty of power to punch her way through the seas. The waves always seem larger at night, and larger still when you're alone, which may be why I tied in the earlier reef. We're still in shelf water and the waves grow more quickly here than in deeper regions. It seems a rude welcome back to the North Atlantic, but fast and straight are fine compensations for a bit of discomfort.

I doze on and off at the nav desk and wake to the chiming of the AIS alarm. The AIS transmits information through a radio signal between two vessels, a technology that has filtered down from commercial shipping to those "recreational vessels" that choose to keep company with the big boys. The receiver on *Rubicon* directs this information to two small screens, one in the cockpit and one at the nav station. If a ship is within range, the ship's name will appear on the screen along with its course, speed, and, of great interest, its CPA, or closest point of approach. The ship's destination is also shown, which is useless information to me but always read with curiosity. I care about its present course far more than its final destination, and particularly the ship's course relative to mine.

Passing ships will also see *Rubicon*'s stats, and if there is uncertainty a radio call can be made. The ability to call a ship by name increases the odds that the call will be acknowledged, and that we will indeed pass in the night. There is no need to call this ship as it looks to pass a few miles behind us. There are rules of the road out here, the COLREGS—International Regulations for Preventing Collisions at Sea—but once away from coastal waters there are no dedicated shipping channels. A steady course, clarity of intent, and vigilance, as well as taking the effort to communicate, will keep you safe—basically the same rules as in a relationship. Another day and the traffic should thin out pretty completely, certainly enough to allow time for sleep.

The obligatory deck inspection is a wet affair, but not difficult. Every morning I take a hands-on, eyes-on, and dialed-in tour to discover any problems that may be brewing. I've stopped being surprised at how frequently things break on a boat. This is true on every boat I've been on, even when I never touched a thing. I've never seen a boat *itself* break, just all of the necessities we've wired, bolted, or glued to the skeleton. This is particularly true of passagemaking, where every 24 hours might equal a month of typical summer use. Wear, chafe, and breakage need to be anticipated, but all looks secure this morning.

In years past, anyone following a race such as the OSTAR would have been limited to the occasional news article from a reporter who had made radio contact with a skipper, or just waited for the race to end to get the story. Now, long-distance sailboat races require that each entrant mount a GPS tracker on his or her vessel. The trackers provide continuous position reports to race headquarters. Anyone with an Internet connection can go to the race website and see where the boats are and what speeds they are making. Incredible! In addition, most of the skippers can e-mail reports, and some are even sending pictures and video. This has allowed solo sailing, once the most isolated of sports, to become a spectator event and has dramatically increased its popularity. However, I don't think any of the boats in this race actually have the ability to connect to the Internet, just the ability to send and receive e-mails through a satellite phone, so you only know your position in the fleet if someone e-mails you that information. Rightly or wrongly, I've been adamant that I want to focus on my own race, rather than on the competitors, so my information flow is limited.

I've enjoyed only one win in an offshore sailboat race, which is perhaps not so bad as this is only my third such race. It was in the double-handed leg of the 2007 Bermuda 1-2 Race from Bermuda to Newport. My partner for the race was my good friend Huw, and we won our class mainly by taking a chance and getting lucky, but also by pushing. We decided to take a more westerly route in anticipation of a favorable eddy in the Gulf Stream. It was mighty lonely when we peeled away from the pack after clearing the buoy off St. George's Harbor. We never did find that favorable current, but we found a wind that allowed us to fly the spinnaker for 32 hours and win our class. That race forged my conviction that in a distance race you need to focus on the weather and your routing, and not confuse the situation with an around-the-buoys race where you absolutely need to watch your competitors closely.

It is still cold despite wool socks, thermal underwear, heavy sweater, foulies, and my seaboots. Bundled up, I feast on oatmeal, slices of bread slathered with peanut butter, and a large mug of tea. The wind is still up and we take one wave in the cockpit. The blue water from the ocean is suddenly cold and clear as it escapes the cockpit and cascades over the transom. The wave has taken last night's cookie crumbs and given the cockpit a good wash. Fortunately breakfast is done, and I manage to save my morning beverage from any saltwater dilution. As I sip my tea I consider how very lucky I am to have the freedom to be out here in this magnificent world of wind, waves, and wonder.

There was a phase I went through, some time after Gail's death. I don't know if it is universal to the process or not, but I imagine it's common. It's that period when you walk around thinking, "I can do whatever I want." It's not that you feel entitled to do any particular thing, just that you have an independent power to choose, and that you could choose from a vast menu of options.

All good marriages require a cornerstone of compromise—compromise that is voluntary and generous in spirit, perhaps even unsolicited, just as St. Paul described in his prize-winning note to those Corinthians. But compromise is compromise and, by definition, it means that you don't do everything you wish to do. The great gift of a successful marriage may be ample reward, but there is, I dared to admit, a certain feeling of freedom that flows when you realize that compromise is no longer required.

To be sure, with children in the picture compromise punctuated every day, but that goes with the territory and—as with most parents—it was territory I wished to travel. *Men in Black* would not have been my personal selection for a Saturday matinee, and until McDonald's rolls out their McScotch and Soda it will never be a preferred haunt, but these are hardly compromises. Nevertheless, on the bigger questions of middle-class American life—career choices, where to live, where to spend vacations, what car to park in the driveway, how family income is budgeted, et cetera—the choices were now mine and mine alone.

Contemplating that freedom was like drinking bad wine. Whatever appeal the first glass might hold, the second is hard to swallow. The more I considered it, the more ersatz it became. Most of the new freedoms failed the "so-what test" right out of the gate, and on others the freedom was a mirage. In the movie *Sleepless in Seattle*, a sweet but flawed story, an architect loses his wife and decides to leave Boston and his extended family for a new beginning in Seattle with his young son. In the real world it would be a cruel man who would respond to the death of his wife by moving to the other side of the country and severing his bereaved son's close connection to his grandparents and friends. I learned in those early years of solo parenting that I could be selfish, but I still had to look in the mirror.

In the evening of that phase, I understood that I had new obligations, commitments, and responsibilities, but precious little new freedom. However, some choices did exist that were mine alone, and sailing was my most egregious.

We move through life as if down a river and the banks frame our options. Sometimes the banks spread wide apart, sometimes they narrow, and in our final moments we sail over the edge of the world. Our responsibility to ourselves, to those we may care about—whether we know them or not—and to whatever force we believe gave us this precious gift, is to understand our options and choose wisely. The price is steep for time spent grieving lost options.

The sound of a flogging sail is a distress cry to any sailor. Flogging will kill a sail, and what is a sailor without sails? Sails are designed to catch and harness the wind, but sometimes the reverse occurs and the sail is left to flap around in the wind, beating itself to death. I hear that cry now, the sound of a row of wet sheets hung from a clothesline and dancing in a thunderstorm. I look forward to see that one of the short lines (ropes) holding up the foot of the reefed solent sail has blown out. As I watch the foot of the sail doing a flap dance on the foredeck, a second line goes. Pretty soon the sail is making a hell of a commotion and I wish, not for the first time, that I could summon rested crew to the foredeck. Ignoring the problem will no doubt lead to a greater annoyance, so I make my way forward where, clipping in and hanging on, I douse the sail and lash it to the high side of the boat. I decide that the storm jib would be the best outfit for the boat to wear with the wind hitting 35 knots and the boat shoving its way through a close formation of ugly black waves, so I drag the storm jib to the foredeck and get it rigged. Fortunately, the hank-on storm jib can be attached right above the hank-on solent sail, so this is accomplished without a great deal of drama, and we are still making a reasonable turn of speed. I had turned downwind to accomplish the foredeck work in a slightly more civilized manner, and on arriving back in the cockpit I put her back on the close-hauled course, trim the storm jib, and sit down to contemplate the achievement. Neglecting to tuck my head under the dodger, I am quickly drenched with spray when the boat hits one of those bully waves. It's always something!

I'm thankful for an article by an earlier OSTAR competitor, Jerry Freeman, who wrote that you just have to gut it out for the first three days till you get away from the traffic and into deep water, and then just keep going and grind out the miles to Newport. It sounds pretty simple when you write it down, though many good strategies are. It's also a familiar strategy for me—just grind out the miles, or the days, and one day you'll wake up and boot camp will be over, or this or that oppressive storm will have passed and the sun will be shining again. Now execution is all that is required. My routing or tactics of course will be dictated by the weather patterns, in particular the steady train of low-pressure systems coming off the East Coast of the United States and making their own unique transatlantic passages.

All of my life I have been plagued by seasickness, but I usually find my sea legs early in the season. I had only one day of queasiness on the passage to Plymouth, and that right at the beginning of the trip. I thought the heavy weather we'd experienced on the passage over, and the short gap between my arrival in Plymouth and the start of the OSTAR, would inoculate me from any bout of seasickness on the return passage. Apparently the vaccination didn't work, or perhaps it was the months of preparation, the hectic week in Plymouth, or just the long night of tracking the many ships aiming for the mouth of the English Channel. Whatever the cause, I'm a bit out of it; not ill exactly, but I can only muster the energy to keep the boat safe and pointing in something approaching the right direction before closing my eyes and resting.

Despite the presence of four comfortable bunks on *Rubicon*, I sleep on the cabin sole (floor), just at the bottom of the compan-

ionway (the steps connecting the cockpit to the boat's interior), where I stretch out on the exercise mat I brought for this purpose. It's comfortable enough, but not so comfortable that you delay in going topside when necessary. In difficult conditions it's not even necessary to take off my foul-weather gear or seaboots. It has been a tiring couple of days, but fortunately there is not a great deal that needs doing right now. The sails are drawing, *Rubicon* is moving well, and I'm stretched out on my mat waiting for the dawn. There's a lot of equipment to monitor and maintain on a boat, and I need to remind myself that I'm on that list. I need to push myself or I won't stay competitive, but I need to go the distance or I've lost completely. Striking that balance is one of the keys. If I can find that balance, while making some smart routing decisions and avoiding any more equipment failures, I'll have a finish to be proud of.

A COURSE CHANGE

When thought becomes excessively
painful, action is the finest remedy.
—SALMAN RUSHDIE

D ay three is on us, a brilliant morning, the sea a tapestry of deep blues, patterned with thousands of golden sparklers. The breeze is down to 17 to 20 knots, *Rubicon* is humming, and we're headed just north of west. After two long nights, the lighter conditions are welcome and my appetite returns as I plow through a bowl of hot oatmeal and a banana before my first cup of tea.

The morning e-mail check brings news of the first two retirements from the race. The early going has been rather rough and equipment is starting to break. *Croisieres*, the fast trimaran that led the fleet down the channel, has returned to Plymouth, as has *Lexia*, the only junk-rigged boat in the race. The variety of boats in this race is quite amazing, but they've all had to deal with the hammering waves of the past two days. I confess to the foxhole thought, "better them than me." Another selfish thought crowds in: if boats need to drop out of the race and return to port, why can't it be the ones I'm racing against, the ones in my class? After selfishness has run its course, I give some thought to the disappointment of the retiring entrants.

Having the ability to communicate on a sailboat hundreds of miles offshore strikes me as a remarkable technical feat. I'm old enough to remember life without computers, and I still marvel at the incredible utility of these little boxes. My notebook computer is strapped to the top of the nav desk, a flat panel display is mounted behind it, and industrial-strength Velcro secures a mouse and keyboard in their proper locations. There is no Internet access, but I can send and receive e-mails. I write all of my e-mails first, and when I'm done I hit the start button on a program that sends the correspondence out through the satellite phone sitting in a docking station just behind the computer. The messages then travel to the antenna on the stern rail and up to a satellite to be bounced back down to a point onshore where they are forwarded to their final in-boxes. The program then retrieves any e-mails waiting for me on the server and returns them by the same path. This can sometimes make for disjointed conversations, but all in all it's great. Text e-mails from friends are transmitted quickly, but it can take some minutes for the weather charts to download so, as I pay by the minute, I usually put my mind to some other task while this is going on. I can't help but wonder what the sailors who raced in the first OSTAR in 1960 would have thought about this capability: a wonderful aid to safety and enjoyment, or an unwelcome intrusion into the purity of life on an ocean passage?

The day unfolds with a strategically problematic wind shift to the west. This means that I must go farther north to get any westing, but I have determined that I don't want to go that far north. I expect the winds to shift more to the southwest overnight—in fact, they are grudgingly starting to do that now—so that will help greatly, and of course it goes with the program. I'm jogging along slowly, pointing too close to the wind, as I ponder the current realities. Finally, the reality that hits me is that I'm breaking one of the first rules of sailboat racing—go *somewhere* fast.

Unbelievably, the generator has died only a minute into its daily run to charge the batteries. Incredibly frustrating, as this was one problem I thought had been put to bed in Plymouth, where an excellent mechanic found a disintegrating gasket in the fuel tank. Pieces of semibuoyant rubber were found floating in the tank, periodically blocking the fuel intake. As there was no time to fully drain and clean the tank, I can only think that there may be additional bits of rubber causing mischief in the tank. Whatever the cause, it will likely be hard to remedy at sea. This is another of the lessons in patience brought to me by the wonderful world of sailing.

With the generator out of action, I turn to the main engine to get the daily charging program underway. The generator is more efficient at charging, but the main engine can do the job and it's perfectly allowable as long as you are running in neutral solely to charge your batteries. The engine fires up instantly but when I push the button on the throttle/gear handle to keep the engine out of gear while I increase the revs, the handle feels loose in my hand. I discover that the inside of the handle has sheared and I can, and do, slide the unit right out of its sleeve and deposit it in my pocket. I have no idea how this happened. I never saw any of the lines wrapped around the handle, though that would be the most probable cause. There are indeed a lot of lines in the cockpit, including preventers, runners, two sets of jib sheets, the mainsheet, the jib furler line, and traveler lines. A spaghetti of strings to control the size and shape of the sails, the only engine that will drive *Rubicon* on this passage.

This latest bit of breakage will also go unaddressed till we reach port as I don't have a replacement throttle control unit. You have to draw the line somewhere when bringing spare parts! I now have no way of putting the engine in gear, or controlling the throttle, and I will need some docking assistance when I arrive in Newport, or anywhere else if I decide to bail. It is possible to perform a docking under sail, or to sail onto a mooring, but completing these maneuvers singlehandedly can be tricky. *Rubicon* handles like a dream when she has way on (i.e., when she is moving), but at very slow speeds with little water passing the rudder, her 44 feet and 28,000 pounds are slow to respond. A little aggressive engine control while docking can make the difference between a smooth landing and an insurance claim.

Given today's problems, I very briefly consider a retirement from the race and a retreat back to Plymouth. I mull the idea while eating half a bar of chocolate and staring at the chart and quickly conclude that I'm being very silly. I have no need to put the engine in gear, and I will need a tow for the final yards to the dock wherever I wind up. As far as battery charging, many of the boats in the race don't even have diesel generators, though many do have solar panels or wind generators as a backup to their engines for battery charging. I can still charge the batteries from the engine, and it has always been very reliable. The problem is only a potential one. I am now on my backup charging system. If the engine should join the disabled list, the batteries would gradually drain and there would be no electrical power on *Rubicon*. It's amazing how many energy hogs there are on a modern boat—autopilot, chartplotter, navigation lights, communications, and instruments, not to mention the stereo and refrigeration. However, *Rubicon* has a large battery bank thanks to the four new batteries I installed in the spring, and if necessary I could adopt *Apollo 13*-type conservation measures, which should allow me to maintain limited use of basic instruments and power up for daily communications. Inconvenient, but doable.

An hour passes while I thaw a frozen dinner from the icebox, fire up the stove, and rifle though my CDs. Savoring a plate of hot lasagna and listening to Patsy Cline singing of the pain of life and love, today's irritations lose their sting and my mind drifts back to when I first determined to take up solo sailing.

The idea to take up solo ocean sailing was born late on a January evening in 1998, as I sat in my study reading sailing magazines. From the moment of birth, its vital signs were strong and it only grew, adding definition and substance. Specifically, my idea was to buy a sailboat, learn it as any musician learns his instrument, fit it out, provision it, and sail it to Bermuda and back, completing the return leg alone. Some friends viewed this as a foolhardy plan. I knew that it would not be without some risk, but if done right it would certainly not be foolhardy. It would, however, be a high challenge and a great adventure.

As a young boy I experienced a nine-day Atlantic crossing on the good ship *Fairsea*, a British liner engaged in the immigrant trade. I was on my way to America, the second child in a family from England. As a young man I crossed the Pacific, or most of it anyway, in a sixteen-day passage on an LSD (landing ship dock), a navy troop and cargo ship. It was a slow passage from Da Nang,

Vietnam, to Pearl Harbor, Hawaii, but the small group of happy marines didn't mind the pace. These ocean transits made indelible impressions on me, but they are nothing like driving your own boat.

I have always been fascinated by ocean sailing, though my only on-deck experience to that point had been as a supernumerary on a short delivery from New Jersey to Rhode Island. That two-day passage, on a meticulously maintained Morgan 45, taught me that ocean sailing can be cold, wet, exhausting, and, if you're not used to it, nauseating. The accumulated wisdom from decades of armchair sailing, reading of the great and not so great ocean passages, had always been gathered while warm and dry. Wet or dry, hot or cold, sailing had become my sport of choice.

About a year after I lost Gail, I realized, quite clinically, that I needed to find something besides work and parenting. Life and circumstance had left me working flat out trying to maintain my professional position, be a good father, and keep everything together. At the late-night end of many days, I found myself mumbling: "I can't keep doing this, this is killing me, I'm dying." It wasn't a question of wanting out of the parenting role, or the business role, but I needed a third ball for balance. I wanted to keep the oath I repeatedly made at Gail's graveside, that I would be the best father I knew how to be. But being yet another (more or less) educated, late-twentieth-century specimen of the species, I wanted more. I wanted my career, which I had spent years building, to continue. I wanted travel, which had never before been oppressive in its requirements, to continue. I wanted this. I wanted that. I had all the self-actualization goals viewed as entitlements by my generation, yet for the moment, I would settle for one great adventure.

Bermuda was an obvious choice, not because it was the honeymoon destination where Gail and I enjoyed the opening days of our marriage, though that was a nice confluence of circumstances, but simply because of where it is on the globe. At latitude 32° N and longitude 64° W, Bermuda is approximately 640 nautical miles from New York. It is far enough to qualify as a true blue-water ocean passage, yet near enough to make the trip within the parameters of a corporate vacation allowance. It was the only destination that made any sense. The other, and equally real, answer is that the project would consume my mind, and whatever energies remained after my duties as father and breadwinner had registered their cumulative debits. It would be an overflow valve and it would be in place through my personal segue into the new millennium. If I could work such alchemy as to channel rage and frustration into energy for this project, I concluded that I could actually do it. I thought that by the time I tied up to the dock at the end of the passage, I would have figured out a way to move on with my life.

So, in the fall of 1999, I bought a boat, and I no longer felt that I was sinking. I did the Bermuda passage in June 2001, alone in one sense, but with the help of many people, and it was grand. I think it did help me move on with my life, and to enjoy the years that followed where sailing took a back seat, but I could not escape the realization that I was still infected with the solo sailing bug. I didn't succumb to the lure again until the children were grown, or at least graduated from high school, but it was not out of my system.

It's still cold and I'm wearing the thermals that I put on before the start of the race and foul-weather pants. It's no longer raining, but they keep me warm and it always seems to be wet up forward. I'm also snug in a heavy wool sweater from Ireland and the watch cap with the NYC logo. I search in vain for the new sunglasses I splurged on back in Newport. They are nowhere to be found, so I put on the old ones with the duct tape repair to the damage of an earlier footfall when I was being my usual clumsy self.

The wind has continued to shift and is now out of the south, allowing *Rubicon* to return to a directionally approved groove. The always unappealing prospect of retreat is now an old memory, and it's on to Newport!

AN INAUSPICIOUS BEGINNING

*Failure is only an opportunity to
begin again more intelligently.*

—HENRY FORD

A freshly baked fruitcake, well wrapped in tinfoil and enclosed in a zippered bag, sits tucked into a nook in the galley. Johnny Carson once joked that there was only one fruitcake in the country and it was simply passed around every year from person to person. Fruitcake has never been wildly popular in the States, but I have always loved this crazy food concoction, where I like to think that I'm having a healthy meal, five of the four required food groups and dessert all at the same time. This fruitcake was a parting gift from friends in Plymouth, but came with the admonition that I not cut into it until I reach the halfway point. Sailing, or life itself, is nothing without a code of honor, and observing the little things is good exercise for the real tests.

Today's inspection reveals two clutch problems, but easily repairable ones. A clutch on a boat is a kind of jammer that will stop and hold a line. Without them, you would be constantly tying and untying knots as you take in lines or ease them out. The spring in the mainsheet clutch has come off and the jib reefing line clutch has jammed. Sheets are the principal lines controlling the shape of a sail, so the mainsheet controls the mainsail. A few minutes with the needle-nose pliers, a new spring, and some lubricant and both pieces of gear are once again back in the program. As usual, I feel an outsized satisfaction from this minor boat work.

All competitors in distance sailing events know well how to read weather from a chart or from the sky, but those who can tease out the opportunities to catch a tailwind or avoid a roadblock, and have the energy and aggressiveness to go after them, are often the ones digging out the blue blazer for a podium appearance. I've been studying the 48- and 96-hour surface analysis charts showing highs, lows, and fronts, and the associated wind and wave forecasts. Just as those living on the East Coast of the United States can see their weather systems coming as they track from west to east across the continent, so too can sailors see their weather tracking across the Atlantic as the earth continues to spin on its axis. In the Northern Hemisphere, all low-pressure systems, or depressions, bring winds that circulate counterclockwise around their centers. Therefore, the advantage goes to those sailors who can maneuver to get the wind from behind or on their beams or, failing that, at least get out of the way. Being on the wrong side of these systems can mean a slow, bumpy slog to windward, and possibly damaging winds. Sometimes the system is too big, the boat too slow, or the diversion too great to obtain ideal positioning, and there is nothing for it but to grit your teeth and fight your way through. Depressions, like snowflakes, are unique and each low brings its particular combination of size, shape, speed, strength, path, and longevity. Watching these systems march, meander, or maraud across the seas, and anticipating the contours of their short careers, brings the art to the routing side of ocean sailing.

I haven't had any update on my position relative to the fleet since a very early e-mail from a friend saying that I was well forward within my class. I'm curious, but I'm going to keep my focus on the boat I'm sailing, and we'll see what it looks like in Newport. The idea of winning line honors, of being the first boat into Newport, has never entered my speculations; there are much faster boats in the race, and far more experienced skippers. The potential to do well within my class is another matter. The great sailor Giovanni Soldini said, "Race the weather, not your competitors," so my goal is to see what others miss in the charts and find that opening for a faster passage. However, I wrestle little of great threat or value from today's hour of staring at the charts with all their squiggly lines. I have no illusions about my own abilities as a weather forecaster. My confidence is basically capped at a belief that I can keep the boat from being in the proverbial wrong place at the wrong time. There is one rather large and deep low-pressure system in the eastern Atlantic, but it looks to be tracking toward Iceland and should be a nonevent.

It will be noon soon, and that is when I note my position and record the 24-hour run, the distance from Plymouth, and the distance to Newport; besides the race, there is a fruitcake riding on this. The race committee also requires that you communicate your noon position each day via e-mail or sat(ellite) phone. This is a bit redundant as the tracking device reports your position, but it serves the useful purpose of confirming that someone is actually on the boat.

Sometimes I just look around the boat and smile at the good fortune I've had to be here, and how unlikely it would have seemed to anyone who knew me not so many years ago. I was already middle aged before I was able to master a Sunfish, though even that exercise was ocean sailing.

I had been sitting on the beach all morning watching my children play as they enjoyed the spring break from their middle school in New Jersey. I had also been watching my fellow vacationers at Jamaica's Boscobel resort take out the small Sunfish sailboats. The location was idyllic, on the north coast and located right in the path of the trade winds. Blue sky, white sandy beach, and sparkling aqua water gave the look of a postcard to a glorious day.

Conditions were quite breezy on this fourth day of our family vacation. I dearly wanted to take a boat out, more to begin my training than for the fun quotient, yet I knew I didn't really have the skill set. This was two months before the scheduled beginning of my formal sailing education in Newport, so I contented myself in watching the various attempts of the other guests. Success was about fifty-fifty. A few skilled sailors were doing well and obviously having fun. Others were capsizing within minutes. I watched as scientifically as I could, trying to note where mistakes were being made and what was working. As Yogi Berra might have said, you can see a lot just by watching. Perhaps not enough though.

By early afternoon, with the winds somewhat abated, I had convinced myself that I could probably handle the conditions and strolled down to the boats. As luck would have it, another lone "sailor" arrived at the same time and we decided to team up. We both admitted to being novices, yet each somehow felt the other possessed some unrevealed level of skill. That illusion was to have a brief life.

One of the delightful aspects of sailing is that you can generally sail from any point A to any point B regardless of which way the wind is blowing. The time-and-energy-consuming catch is that you can't always go in a straight line, and depending on the wind's direction, there can be many and distant points between A and B, but as long as there is wind, you needn't drift.

The sail started out well enough, and we sorted out our individual responsibilities of steering and sail trimming. Unfortunately, we had too little momentum as we entered what was to be our final tack. Whether you tack from port or starboard, the act of tacking to the opposite side involves turning the bow through the wind. The boat will lose momentum as soon as you turn it head to wind because this shuts off the usable wind. The fuel valve is closed until you complete the turn and the sails catch the wind on the opposite side. Failing to complete the turn before the friction of the water and the absence of usable wind bring the boat to a halt leaves the boat drifting. "Caught in irons" is the old nautical term for this condition. You are indeed caught, like a boat in a mooring field, face to the wind, stopped and resting until you can coax the bow around, harness some wind, and resume sailing.

This will explain my chagrin at being caught in irons, particularly as this discovery came just as we realized our close proximity to the submerged reef and its unadvertised undertow. Events then moved rather quickly, and we soon found ourselves over the reef and being hit by surprisingly large waves. At least they were surprisingly large compared with how sedate they had appeared from the beach. Before we could regain headway, a wave caught us, capsizing our little vessel and throwing us into the water. The waves seemed even larger from this vantage point, and they were now crashing over us. I knew the drill, at least in theory. First, make sure the daggerboard is fully extended, and then use it to lever the boat back to an upright position. This is a very difficult maneuver to accomplish when you are being assaulted by waves.

Unfortunately, we had exhausted our nautical competence for the day, and after a few failed attempts to right our craft we saw evidence that today's adventure would soon be over. Our mainsail was rapidly floating away from the boat! I did a little mental math. The reef was visible 6 to 8 feet down. The boat had a 20-foot mast. The boat was upside down. Even in a situation not conducive to reasoned analysis, the conclusion was clear. The mast was gone! Indeed, when we later examined the boat, we saw that the mast had broken off at the base. Putting aside for the moment the resort's damaged Sunfish, the only losses were my Orlando Magic Cap and my favorite pair of Ray-Bans. We had the good sense to stay with the boat, and before long two of the resort's staff were powering their way to us on a Jet Ski. Two young and skilled Jamaicans did an admirable job of towing us back to the beach, and an even more admirable job of hiding their disdain for these two buffoons who had just dismasted their boat. To my great surprise, the manager did not want or accept what would have been a very justified surcharge. The worst part, of course, was wading ashore and returning our life jackets to the rack. The beach chairs were fully occupied, and we had been the main event that afternoon. It was clear that my sailing skills could most charitably be described as embryonic.

To capsize and dismast a Sunfish was a very inauspicious beginning to my recently set goal, one that was a very long way from being even a reasonable stretch goal. Ocean sailing on a Sunfish in reef-infested waters was something I was not yet ready for, and it had been a stupid decision to attempt it. From now on I would need to learn faster and decide better. For a while I was in a funk, viewing the exercise as a failure, but within a few hours I had come to view it as a stepping-stone. It was both. Shortly afterward my children returned from an afternoon of kid activities at the resort. Amy looked very cute in her new Jamaican braids. They were happy and didn't ask about my afternoon, and I may have forgotten to tell them.

There are two long bench seats on either side of *Rubicon*'s cockpit where you can sit or stretch out and catch a nap. There is also a helm seat behind the wheel, no good for sleeping or even sitting in heavy weather when you need your feet braced and steering is a stand-up job, but today it is a sweet perch. From here I can see the set of the sails. I can also see the row of instruments over the companionway. These show our boat speed, the wind's speed and direction, and our course. The final instrument shows water depth, but this has no readout now. Once the depth exceeds 300 feet, the readouts stop.

Deep water is a relative term. Within a half hour of the start, the water was too deep for the anchor to reach the seabed, and the anchor is now stowed to keep the weight off the front of the boat. The continental shelf is well behind us and we're in blue water, where the depths approach the ocean average of 2 miles. To say one is "in deep water" implies one is in a situation somewhere between uncomfortable and precarious. So far I've experienced only the near end of that range, which is fine with me.

Hours roll by, hunger builds, and the light fails as I revel in our progress while the peace of here builds. It is a busy peace though, as I tweak the sails to coax out that next elusive increment of boat speed.

GOING SOLO

Being entirely honest with oneself is a good exercise.
—SIGMUND FREUD

For the second day clouds blanket the sky from rim to rim, and the light filtering through their layered formations dapples the seascape with cold and beautiful grays. These seas do not threaten, their wave heights are modest, and the stronger winds of the night have eased, but they are serious seas and hold no hint of invitation. The world seems very different from the glittering vistas of two days ago, which seemed so welcoming as we sailed on. Once over the horizon and away from the coastal traffic, you're in wilderness territory. It has not escaped the hand of man, as witnessed by the reports of decimated fish stocks or the occasional piece of floating plastic, but you can sail for days and not see any of those fingerprints. It looks and feels as it must have looked and felt ten thousand years ago, had there been anyone to bear witness. It is a wild place, though it often wears a benign countenance. Despite the somber seas, I am in good spirits and breakfast has moved to the top of the agenda. I dive into the galley and scramble three eggs. Add a can of corned beef hash and a splash of ketchup, and I'm halfway to heaven. A pot of fresh coffee, Sarah Vaughan soaring from the cockpit speakers, and I'm the rest of the way.

Sailors learn that the guiding rule for when to reef is to do it when you first think about it. Weather that is heavy, as sailors say, and getting heavier, will rarely pause to allow the delinquent seaman time to reef his sails in an orderly manner. Last night, as *Rubicon* was barreling along at 8 to 9 knots, I found reasons to ignore this rule. I was tired from a long day of working the boat, and the speed was intoxicating. Sloth and greed are two of the seven deadly sins as I recall, and sinners eventually receive the bill. In my case it came quickly when the wind started piping over 30 knots.

Early in the night I had rolled up the big genoa (a.k.a. the genny), put one reef in the main, and set the storm jib. This was relatively easy as the storm jib was already hanked to the inner forestay. A sail hank is a type of shackle, one end of which is permanently attached to the forward edge of a sail. The other end of the hank has a ring on it with a quick opening mechanism that allows the ring to be closed around the forestay, a strong wire cable running from the deck to a high point on the mast. Once all the hanks are attached, the sail is "hanked on" and ready for action. All I had to do was go to the bow, release the sail ties securing the sail on the deck, go to the winch at the mast to raise the sail, and hustle back to the cockpit to winch in the jib sheet and sculpt the form to function. I accomplished all this without trouble, scurrying like a horseshoe crab, keeping low and holding on.

Around one in the morning the breeze was still building, and sailing close to the wind *Rubicon* was complaining loudly of both too much canvas and an unbalanced rig. The storm jib was an excellent headsail for the conditions, but the big main needed to be lowered to the next reef point. There was nothing for it but to put on the foulies and harness and go on deck. As it was pretty wet up by the mast, I turned *Rubicon* downwind for the maneuver, which made life a lot flatter and drier. This would have been an intelligent move, except that the time for the more civilized approach had passed. Unfortunately this didn't stop me from trying it. I lowered the halyard almost far enough to get to the second reef point when the mainsail didn't want to go down anymore. The sail was pressed hard against the mast spreaders. When I shone a light on it, the mainsail looked like it was in a wet T-shirt competition as the sailcloth pressed against the spreaders. My first reaction was, "Oh shit, if I've torn the main, just finishing the OSTAR will be tough." My second reaction was, "Ooooooohhh shiiiiiit, if the main gets snagged on the spreaders it's going to be a nasty bit of work climbing up there to free the sail." I gently headed the boat upwind a few degrees and the sail lifted from the spreaders like a sheet from a bed. It's moments like this that tempt one to believe that there really is a benevolent God who takes an interest in our affairs and lends a helping hand from time to time. I quickly secured the second reef and, as usual, *Rubicon* was going just as fast with the extra reef, but much more in control.

Businesspeople often refer to the "takeaway" from a meeting. My takeaway from last night's experience was "reef when you first start thinking about it," just like it says in the learn-to-sail books.

It is the rare day when every cylinder in your life is firing to spec and, other than that little clusterfumble with the mainsail one hour into the day, all cylinders are now firing.

The day rushes by as *Rubicon* rushes west, all reefs out now and the full main and genoa powering us along. We both seem to be savoring the experience, *Rubicon* being where she was built to be and doing what she was designed to do.

This race is my third offshore solo sail. In 2001, less than three months before 9/11, I sailed *Steadfast* from New Jersey to Bermuda with friends and did the return voyage solo. In 2007, I sailed *Rubicon* from Newport to Bermuda in the solo leg of the Bermuda 1-2 Race. Before my first solo adventure I tried hard to analyze the decision, and used only those rationalizations absolutely necessary to the project.

I told friends that I wasn't out to prove anything to anyone, but an honest answer would admit that I did view it as a qualifying exam. If I could do this, then I must be at least a reasonably competent sailor, a qualified sailor, and I had needed to start something new and just get good at it. During my many years as an armchair sailor I read the sagas of the great sailors (Joshua Slocum, Bernard Moitessier, Vito Dumas, Naomi James, Alain Colas, and many others) and inhaled the spirituality of solo sailing. A solo blue-water sail was on my short list of life goals. Finally, and fundamentally, solo sailing is a retreat, albeit a very busy one, and that is what I needed. I desperately wanted a retreat from my day-to-day concerns to a space where I might put my life in some perspective. To solo or not to solo was a question I wrestled with for a long time. On a few occasions I abandoned the idea of the solo leg, but each time it seemed that the purpose of the trip had been severely compromised, and preparations resumed.

I am a believer in the team approach to many things, and my great disappointment in life is that I had to play so many years of the Parenting Olympics, the games to which every parent is invited to compete, with half the team gone. There are, however, some things in life that must, at least sometimes, be done solo. Sailing with crew is grand fun and can be a huge adventure. Solo sailing is not better, or worse, than sailing with a crew. It is a singular experience in every sense. It is a total immersion in the life. It is the visit to a monastery, and it changes you.

To be at sea is to be in a different world, and to live alone for a time in this alien place can yield a spiritual calm. The attraction is no doubt similar to that felt by the religious hermits who sought their land-based hermitages in remote corners. In such a calm, order and perspective can enter your thoughts (followed, in the case of the hermits, by a life of devotion). Life can be harsh at sea, but it is never sordid. The simple necessities of food, drink, and sleep are received with gratitude, and always there is the sea's reminder that you are a speck of dust in the cosmos. The rush of thoughts slows, and order replaces the chaos as you consider your journey.

Solo sailing can be a controversial topic. We are talking here about sailing where you are away from shore for days or weeks at a time, not just an afternoon. It was interesting to me that the two people most responsible for my development as a sailor, and both of them better seamen than I'll ever be, were on opposite sides of this debate. Kevin left no doubt of his position, telling me in a friendly but emphatic tone, "It's flat-out illegal and you're fucking nuts to consider it." To my great benefit, he became an enthusiastic and invaluable supporter the moment he realized he could not dissuade me from the endeavor. Hank was on the other side of the issue. He spoke with enthusiasm of his solo sail from Long Island to Spain on his Tayana 37, and was totally supportive of my venture.

There are three issues in the singlehanded sailing debate: legality, prudence, and morality. The legal stickiness enters in when consideration is made of rule 5 of the COLREGS. This rule stipulates that "every vessel shall at all times maintain a proper look-out by sight and hearing as well as by all available means appropriate in the prevailing circumstances and conditions so as to make a full appraisal of the situation and of the risk of collision."

In the days before technology made its great leap forward in the boating world, rule 5 seemed crystal clear. Today, with the increased sophistication of systems for collision avoidance, dramatic improvements in both active and passive watch-keeping capabilities have developed. To what degree the electronic eyes may be viewed as substitutes for the human eye depends on whom you talk to. When I cleared Bermuda immigration I had to stipulate the number of crew on board (one) and the authorities had no objection, just as the U.S. Coast Guard had no problem with my solo status when I returned to the United States. Given the number of international singlehanded sailboat races, many receiving active support from various governments, it is fair to say that governments have made their peace with singlehanded sailing.

At this point in time the regulatory regime is go if you want to, and no doubt a large reason for this attitude is that any risk presented is almost entirely shouldered by the solo sailor. On any collision between a ship and your typical sailing yacht, there will be no damage to the ship. There have even been cases where ships have run down sailboats and never noticed. It would be like a collision between a jogger and a building. The building will be fine.

In terms of prudence, there is no doubt that the more conservative approach when doing any ocean passage is to ally yourself with a competent crew, or at least one other experienced sailor. I am a conservative person when it comes to risk, but I do believe that everyone has a "risk budget," and conscious budgeting decisions are a worthwhile endeavor. I believe in the value of probability as a guide, so I tend to view the risks you take as you go through life from a budgeting perspective, balancing risk and reward. I have tried to teach my children about risk—avoid all risk and you'll have a very pale life; accept stupid risks and you may have a very short life. We each have to determine what risks make sense, and when to take a pass.

Ocean sailing in general, and singlehanded sailing in particular, carries a number of risks; some have lessened over the years and some have increased. The equipment on a modern yacht, including boat-handling equipment (roller-furling headsails, self-tailing winches), navigation equipment (GPS, weather fax), and safety equipment (radar, AIS alarms, EPIRBs, satellite phones), makes singlehanded sailing easier and safer. On the other side of the coin are ships. There are more of them than ever before, they run faster than ever before, and they have smaller crews than ever before. You may go for days and not see a ship, but I have seen one that is a barely visible speck on the horizon come to my little neighborhood in the time it takes to prepare a decent sandwich. Some ships have

only one person on watch at night, and that is from inside a high bridge. If the ship's electronics are down, you'll be lucky if anyone sees you, not to mention that a ship can easily travel 5 miles while the person on watch is taking a leak.

The moral issue is the difficult one, but as risks will always exist in the offshore world, it must be addressed. To start, there is the risk of putting the lives of rescuers in peril if you need to call on them in difficult conditions. The only proper way to mitigate this risk is to build your competence to the point where you are highly confident that you can meet the challenges of the voyage. I would call the fire department if my house were on fire, and if the mast were to come crashing down leaving me injured and unable to work the boat, I would no doubt reach for my EPIRB, but it's my responsibility to keep both of those probabilities remote.

Whatever one's skill level, it is valid to pose the question of whether an individual has the right to put their life at risk to achieve a purely personal goal. In particular, do parents with dependent children have that right? Of course, people do just that every day, in behaviors ranging from drug taking to mountain climbing to smoking to a thousand other activities. Was it a conceit to think that this issue had some special significance for me? No. The risks involved, the duration of the commitment, and the depth of my responsibilities as a single parent made it an issue I could not escape, though I hid from it as long as I could. The bottom line for me came down to Amy and Steven. I did have to return. If not for them, I would have had no moral conflict over the solo decision, but they were still only thirteen and fifteen in 2001. How could I take that chance?

In the early spring of 2001 I realized that I had painted myself into a box where there were only two options. Abandon the adventure that had been an inspiration for over three years, or commit to taking a risk that was fundamentally incompatible with my primary responsibilities as a parent of minor children. Amazingly, I had not wrestled with the question when I first conceived the plan, and in retrospect that seems odd. I think there was a certain unreal quality to the plan, a feeling that it was all a fantasy, a story of Walter Mitty taking up sailing. This allowed me to accept the reassuring voice saying, "Peter, relax, you're never going to get to the starting line on this project," and so the moral complexities of the goal never had the opening they needed for a full hearing.

By the spring of 2001 it was clear that I was rapidly approaching the starting line, and then my conscience said it was time for a chat. I had decided to go. Selfishly perhaps. Well, let's just say selfishly. I could not reconcile the arguments. I simply announced to myself that this would be a one-off. ("Oh, OK," said the judge, "the defendant says it's a one-off. Case dismissed.") I guess I knew this was bogus, but I did take a vow to abstain from any further solo sailing adventures until my children had graduated from high school.

But enough of these ruminations from years ago. I took my hiatus from solo sailing after that first Bermuda transit. I reentered that world two years ago with the Bermuda 1-2 Race, and I'm back in the thick of it now.

After dinner I spend an enjoyable bit of time playing with my tracking spreadsheet. I'm estimating that it will take another twenty days to reach Newport, with a margin of error of three days depending on what winds may blow and perhaps a few other variables. That would give me an ETA of June 18, and I doubt I will have any complaints if this forecast proves accurate. King Neptune has not signed off on my forecast, so it all remains to be seen, but for the moment all of *Rubicon's* critical equipment is working well. After brewing a cup of coffee, I tuck myself into the cockpit to play the "what-if" game. It's an exercise well known to sailors, and involves running through the many and various unpleasant events that might unfold on a passage under sail, and what playbook to follow in each case. How to jury-rig a steering system following a rudder failure, quickly patch the hull after a collision with ocean flotsam, or deal with a blown-out mainsail are only a few of the what-ifs to ponder. Thinking through these scenarios for the umpteenth time should smooth the transition from shock to solution if misfortune arrives before reaching port. The game over, I give *Rubicon* a thorough inspection, and finding nothing amiss, we press on into the night.

REASONS TO QUIT

Age wrinkles the body; quitting wrinkles the soul.
—DOUGLAS MACARTHUR

A front came through last night and left a wonderful present: winds of just the right strength, 15 to 20 knots, and from just the right quarter, and we are sailing fast and true. I feel pumped and a tad cocky as I sip my morning coffee and enjoy the spectacular view from the cockpit. The sun is out, one of its rare appearances since the race began, and shards of sunlight are falling on acres of ocean. Indeed, the moment is quite sublime, and as with all such moments it has a short shelf life.

Suddenly, for no apparent reason, the autopilot (AP) ceases to perform the one job it is here to do: to send orders from its electronic brain to the hydraulic ram unit, which in turn directs *Rubicon's* rudder and steers the compass course instructed. With no one at the helm, the autopilot's failure allows *Rubicon* to "round up" and the bow swings into the wind. Rounding up removes any pressure on the sails, and of course any momentum driving the vessel. We are left wallowing, and the inevitable clatter and confusion ensue. Not wanting to lose a perfectly good cup of coffee, it takes me a moment to get to the helm, where I steer *Rubicon* back to our course. I power down the AP and then power it back up again, the tried-and-true first response whenever a computer is part of the game. I hit the button on the AP control panel and everything is back as it had been 10 minutes before. Hopefully, the unit is now over its fit of pique, but it is yet another reminder of how quickly life on a boat can change, for better or for worse.

This little incident makes me think of the competitors who have been forced out of the race with equipment problems. Heavy weather and gear failures have caused four more of the thirty-one starters to retire from the race and return to Plymouth, reducing the fleet to twenty-five. It takes many months, years really, to prepare for this race, and abandoning the quest would be a bitter pill to swallow. I know from reading their bios that some of the skippers now back in Plymouth were potential winners.

The wind is picking up gradually, so I take a reef in the main and we continue to bound along. After a late lunch of a peanut butter and jelly sandwich and a generous chunk of Jarlsberg cheese, it's time for a much-overdue change of clothing. No sooner have I stripped down to my shorts than *Rubicon* loses her autopilot again. Half-dressed, I race to the helm to get things back in order, but this time cycling the power does nothing and the autopilot stays off. In addition to the autopilot, the instruments on the forward side of the cockpit that show wind speed, course, water depth, and boat speed, are—with the exception of boat speed—as blank as the day they came out of the box. It's sunny, but hardly warm, and I'm starting to shiver, so I engage the Hydrovane steering and go below to get dressed.

With the constant requirements to trim sails, navigate, eat, sleep, and maintain the boat, solo sailors need to have some type of auxiliary steering. Most sailors go with an autopilot, which is a wonderful device. You can set the autopilot to a particular course and the boat will stay on that exact course unless the wind shifts to such a degree that the course cannot be held without adjusting the sails. Of course, your pilot will always labor less if you trim your sails as the wind shifts. There are not many negatives with an autopilot, except for the fact that if its electronic brain gets fried for any reason, and you have not been wise enough to carry an expensive spare, which I was not, then you will not be able to repair it underway. A rule of offshore sailing is that for every item on a boat, the crew must be able to either fix it or live without it. This is why many short-handed sailboats, and many boats in the OSTAR, also have some type of wind-vane steering system.

Rubicon's Hydrovane unit is one of the popular models. These systems will also steer a boat without human intervention, but their operation is fundamentally different. They are purely mechanical devices, and usually with very open architecture, so they are both strong and repairable if need be. Another plus for sailors concerned with the amp-hour accounts in their battery banks, an all-inclusive group offshore, is that wind vanes consume no battery power. On the other hand, they tend to look a bit ungainly bolted on the transom of a beautiful sailboat, rather like putting a roof rack on a Ferrari, but all things considered, they are a fantastic piece of kit, as the Brits would say.

The real limitation of any wind-vane unit is that you cannot set one to steer a definitive and constant course, such as 270 degrees. To use the wind vane, you first trim the sails for a particular course, and then set the wind vane relative to the wind. The wind vane steers the boat at a constant angle relative to the wind, so when the wind direction changes, the course also changes. You are definitely going with the flow. Take a nap or focus on some other project, and when your attention returns you might find yourself sailing merrily along in the wrong direction. Far from the influences of land, the winds are more directionally stable, but it is the rare day when you do not observe the breeze strengthening, falling, shifting, backing, clocking, gusting, or just going fluky for a while.

If the boat's instrumentation includes an electronic compass, you can dial in a course heading and set the off-course alarm to sound if the course changes by, say, ten degrees. This is a nice solution to the problem, and one I was counting on when I installed one of these instruments as a winter project on *Rubicon*. I would employ it now if the instrument would do anything other than light up. At least it must be getting power.

The autopilot has muscle and brains, but is not much of a communicator. The wind-vane steering is all muscle and no brain, but is a wonderful communicator. For it to work well and keep the course you intend, the sails must be trimmed properly; it tends to go on strike if they are not, so as an added bonus, your game improves.

Sailors have the peculiar habit of naming their autopilots and wind vanes, reflecting the close connection felt with these ingenious devices, a virtual crew liberating them from the tyranny of the helm. It strikes me as an animistic gesture and there is nothing wrong with that. Though they invariably name the autopilot Otto, they usually get a bit more creative when naming their wind vanes. I named the unit on my first boat Nic as it was installed in the nick of time before my passage to Bermuda. I know one fellow who named his unit Britney. "Britney steers," he explained. I just call mine Hydro.

It will be very hard to be competitive without the tools I have lost today, particularly the autopilot. The thickening clouds seem to be sucking away my dream of a fast passage, and a wave of nausea sweeps over me as I consider the consequences of this quite revolting development. I'm tempted to reach for the bottle of Talisker whisky the race committee had presented to each competitor in Plymouth, but job one is to conquer my own defeatism. If I slip out of race mode I'll have a slower passage still. The nausea passes. I make a cup of tea and start my detective work wishing, not for the first time, that I had combined some engineering with the economics I studied in college.

As my early investigation into the cause of the autopilot's demise is going nowhere, I hop on deck to put a second reef in the main and set the storm jib. Conditions don't really require a further reduction in sail area, but if I can keep the boat a little flatter it will be a lot easier to dig through the wiring and maybe that is where I will find the problem. I also want to adopt a conservative approach for tonight as I have not practiced with Hydro in the dark—my bad—and the wind speed instrument is also out of commission. It's a little difficult to determine the best sail combination, particularly at night, if you're just guessing about wind strength. After my sail change *Rubicon* is still going over 6 knots through the water. At least the boat speed indicator is still working.

It is getting too dark to proceed so I will call it a day. No doubt it's best to get some rest and take a fresh look at the problem in the morning. Last night I was calculating a respectable if not highly competitive ETA in Newport. It will be a slower slog now, unless I can get lucky and find the cause of this problem. The fact that the instruments as well as the autopilot are affected suggests there is a common cause and it must be here somewhere.

On the positive side, I still have the GPS showing my position, the radio, the AIS for collision avoidance, the compass, and, perhaps most of all, my phantom helmsman, the Hydrovane. We're sailing on a beam reach and Hydro seems happy.

ANGER

Anger is short-lived madness.

—HORACE

There is no more blue sky this morning and no more autopilot, but we are sailing fast and hard to Newport. Thank God for Hydro!

Without Hydro, I would have had to abandon the race when the autopilot failed, and this would have been the correct thing to do. I would now be retreating to England or steering toward the Azores, and even that would be very difficult as you can spend only so many hours at the wheel without becoming exhausted. Hydro is my new best friend and with Hydro, I am still in the game.

Best friend is a term not often used by adult men. If they're lucky, their best friend is their wife, or significant other as we say these days, and if they're that lucky they will usually admit it.

To lose Hydro would be a major loss as we're getting to midocean and even the closest port would be a long way to hand steer. I don't want to think of how many hours of standing at the wheel that would require. I wonder if I would be angry if that happened, only the second of Kübler-Ross's five stages of grief.

Sometime after Gail's death, during a discussion of the five stages of grief for God's sake, my father-in-law told me that he was not angry over his daughter's death. Terribly sad, but not angry. "Because it was no one's fault," he said. But I was angry. Very angry.

Despite the love that endures after "death did we part," a good deal of it was selfish anger. I was angry to be a widower at forty-five. I was angry for our two children. I was angry at the new limits put on my career. I was angry that, once the initial earthquake had passed, few called to check in and ask, "How's it going?" Frankly, I was angry that this was how the story of our marriage ended.

Anger was my companion for many of those days, clinging to me with all its corrosive impact and, just as water will always find the easiest path to a resting place, anger will hone in on its richest target. The target of my anger, much to my surprise, was men. I was also surprised at how quickly my rage could erupt, often in response to the mundane. It began as I strove toward normalcy, one strand of which included inviting friends for dinner as we had always done. Here is one conversation, with names changed to protect the guilty:

"So Fred, how would you guys like to come over for dinner next week?"

"Sounds great, let me put Ethel on the phone. She takes care of the calendar."

I'm thinking, *Fred, you're often a few sandwiches short of a picnic, but why can't you do the freaking calendar for once in your pampered life,* but instead I say, "Take your time, I'll hold."

It was always the same with any couple. Was the calendar some mysterious hieroglyph that only a woman could decipher? Pretty soon I gave up, and it was just as well. I later learned that death and divorce typically trigger a friend rotation as the bonds of friendship cease to bind. I considered myself lucky that some remained after the purge.

Each passing day seemed to bring new evidence that men were absolutely incapable of, well, very much at all. Of course I knew that I had created an unfair caricature, even a ridiculous one, but hey, life is unfair. I think it was Jimmy Carter who made that keen observation on national television, and it worked for me.

Our vacation to Jamaica occurred near the peak of my "man against men" phase. When we boarded the plane I thought of that old joke about the two classes of travel: "first class" and "with children," but it wasn't the case that day. The kids were fun, and excited by the prospect of beaches, swimming, and no homework. Amy was peering out the window while Steven tapped away on his Game Boy.

The flight attendant had just issued the familiar announcement to fasten our seatbelts and put our seats in the upright position. In about half an hour we would be landing at the airport near Montego Bay to begin a week of vacation, staying at the "all-inclusive" Boscobel resort. All-inclusive resorts are essentially medium-security lock-ups for kids, but with chicken fingers and water sports, and I mean this as a compliment. The kids can wander around, but they can't wander off, and there's no shortage of high-fun/low-risk activities to leave them with a smile, a sense of adventure, and, best of all, a fatigue that will usher them to sleep at night. The plan was to balance the hedonism of the resort with day trips exploring the island country.

I was enjoying a book and idly listening in on passenger conversation, as one does on a flight of any duration. Two men were seated on either side of the aisle in the next row forward. They didn't seem to know each other, but were both traveling with their families for vacation and a conversation had emerged to pass the time. Their chat had been drifting along rather aimlessly for some time when my brain was jarred by two lines of dialogue.

"Where are you staying in Jamaica?"

"I have no idea; my wife makes all the arrangements."

I wanted to stand up and scream! In 30 minutes this jerk will be landing in a foreign country with his family and he doesn't even know the name of the hotel they're going to. This clown was not taking his family on vacation; he was being taken on vacation. I was outraged and thought, "What if something happens to his wife? What would he do then?" But of course nothing was going to happen to his wife, other than trading a little sunburn for some family memories. Had I voiced the rude question that formed in my mind, and had he taken the high road and responded to a question that was no business of mine, he would likely have said that he had worked his ass off all year to afford this vacation for his family and that was enough. That's a man for you. They can work hard, but once away from the office, the shop floor, or wherever else they go to keep drawing a salary, they revert to their natural form, which is essentially senseless and useless.

It can be very helpful to analyze what's actually going on when you find yourself really angry. I did nothing of the sort.

Compared with the parenting roles I observed growing up, I considered myself a very hands-on father, a full and active partner in raising my children, not the tagalongs that I was seeing all around me. It was still a puzzle that for so many years I had been largely unaware of the glaring difference in gender capabilities. They say that hindsight is 20/20, but that is not always true. There is a mist that falls over the past and we can often see the contours of the thing but not the thing itself.

Being a man of a progressive nature, and for that matter being a man at all, my blatantly biased view eventually started to wear thin, so one day I decided to do all the research time allowed. This meant talking to Mary, a friend and one of my fellow partners at a small investment firm in New Jersey. Mary was a single mom and she always seemed able to cut through the clutter around issues to an understanding of the core. So one morning I walked into her office and asked her to explain to me why women, in general of course, did such a better job at parenting. She gave me the look typically reserved for the slower kids in class, and explained that when women get together they talk about children and parenting, not exclusively, but not reservedly, and they learn from each other and support each other. When men get together, the kid discussion is usually limited to "How are the kids?" "Fine." And then the talk turns to sports or business or whatever. It was a simple truth and revealing. It's not that men love their children any less; it's just the way their minds work. I don't know if it's genetic, but the programming is pretty robust.

I now understand why it is more often the husband who refers to his spouse as his "better half." It seems complimentary, but as working women still do 75 percent of the housework, perhaps their husbands should refer to them as their "better three-quarters." OK, it sounds ridiculous, but realities often are. In custody battles, the tip of the scale of justice usually goes to the mother, and this is because the courts, and society, understand that if the team is down, the smart money will be on the mother as the most valuable player.

My anger finally burned itself out, and fortunately I never got to the point where changing my gender affiliation was a temptation. I did get to the point where I reluctantly admitted that when I still had Gail as my wife, I just might have behaved in ways not totally at odds with a few of the behaviors I now observed with such repugnance. When my angry phase was well past, I grew to appreciate the new perspective I'd gained and to take joy in aspects of parenting that had not been in my job description before, such as clothes shopping for the kids. I don't know if the angry phase was necessary, and it certainly wasn't pretty, but it did eventually lead to a better place.

Single parents can do a superb job. The evidence is in, and I've seen it—they can and they do. I know also that the many and profound joys of parenting are not limited only to the partnerships, but I will always see parenting as a job designed for two, or perhaps even for a village as some have suggested. Is it just that it ain't as much fun solo, or the fact that it's a lot harder? Yes and yes, and one of the ways it's harder is that once you get beyond the single child you're outnumbered. It is no longer politically correct to view parenting as an adversarial relationship, but I absolutely enjoyed it more when the odds were on my side; when I had a wing man, or, more accurately, when I was the wing man.

Even now, embroiled in the challenge of the OSTAR, I know it is the proverbial walk in the park compared to solo parenting. That was a challenge I embraced out of love to be sure, and, as fortune dictated, out of necessity. We play the hands we are dealt.

No luck on solving the autopilot problem, but at least we're still making good time. It's been a tiring day trying to track down the gremlins bedeviling the boat's electronics, trimming sails, and adjusting Hydro, but it goes with the program. It's starting to blow again, and I'm putting a reef in for the overnight hours. I doubt it will slow us down much in this breeze.

SAILING WITH CHILDREN

Children have never been very good at listening to their elders, but they have never failed to imitate them.

—JAMES BALDWIN

You can find the wind's direction by looking up at the swinging needle at the top of the mast, or from its feel on your face, and you can get a sense of the wind's strength from the sea state, the wave action, and the boat's performance, but hard data is always nice. Along with the autopilot and most of the boat's instrumentation, the GPS feed to the chartplotter is also out, so no catalog of information on speed over ground, tracking error, and distances to waypoints. None of this is essential out here, but this is a race, not simply a passage, so this information would have been damn useful. Oh well, fewer numbers to clutter up the mind, but I do admit to missing the visual of the little boat icon doing its slow march across the Atlantic on the chartplotter. The little *x*'s that I write on the paper chart will be sufficient, a method sailors have used for centuries. Curiously, the GPS feed to the radio still works. This is fortunate as I can simply glance at the radio every few hours when I plot my position on the paper chart. No need to power up the handheld unit. Also welcome is the fact that nothing is amiss with the computer or the sat phone, so e-mail is still working, and today's check-in delivers encouraging words from the kids.

A rushed breakfast and then it's back on deck to continue my new relationship with Hydro. I installed the unit just before leaving Newport as a sensible precaution in case my autopilot ever walked out on me. A prudent mariner would have used the eastbound passage to become an expert on sailing with a wind-vane steering system, and those were indeed my intentions. In fact, the passage over was a watery road paved with good intentions. The basics were mastered, but I never continued that education in challenging conditions or during the long dark hours of the night watch. We hand steered for the practice or the sheer joy of it, or we used the autopilot, which we could set and forget, and it was cold, cold, cold on the crossing and the autopilot didn't seem to mind. We were a crew of three, so we also had the luxury of sleep and the pleasures of good conversation. Excuses abound, but now, suddenly, I need Hydro and so I must put in the hours to complete my education.

The wind is up now, easily in the mid-30s with perhaps a few gusts over 40 knots, and we're just humming. Relief has given way to euphoria with the growing realization that the harder it blows, the smoother we're racing along. Hydro is steering flawlessly and demands only that the boat be balanced. The sail plan has to be right, rather like putting the proper shirt with the right pants, and sometimes it can take a couple of wardrobe changes to get it coordinated. We're running in storm dress—triple-reefed main and the storm jib—with the wind just behind the beam, and it feels great. I'm reminded of the famous last line in *Casablanca*: "I think this is the beginning of a beautiful friendship."

When I took delivery of *Rubicon* in the fall of 2004, I had only the vague notion that I would one day do a transatlantic. I was aware of the OSTAR, but I wasn't ready to consciously connect the dots. Today, as I look around *Rubicon*, I know that I bought her for this race.

Steadfast, my first boat, was purchased in Rock Hall, Maryland, and I kept her there for a year. The Chesapeake Bay is a national treasure, with countless cruising destinations from the buzz of Annapolis to the quiet beauty of the Rappahannock River. A finer place to build sailing skills is hard to imagine. You have to keep a weather eye out, but I worried more about grounding than getting caught in bad weather. The Chesapeake has a lot of "thin water," and with *Steadfast* requiring a depth of only 5 feet to stay afloat, it should not have been a major problem to keep her off the bottom. I reasoned that a slow grounding in the muddy bottom of the Chesapeake was unlikely to cause any damage, and during my first season wearing a captain's hat I ran a series of experiments to confirm that hypothesis. As all seamen know, there are three types of sailors: those who have grounded their boats, those who will, and liars.

After that first year, I moved *Steadfast* to a mooring in Raritan Bay, New Jersey. Despite the lure of the Chesapeake, New Jersey was our home and it was the proper mooring for the boat. No more long hours stuck in Sunday traffic, no grumbling from the kids that I was keeping them from their friends for the entire weekend, and no need to dock. I could pick up the mooring with far more finesse—well, success anyway—than I could land at a dock. I disliked using bad language in front of the children, but my embryonic docking skills always required voluble and creative swearing. In one ludicrous moment I told the kids that these words had different meanings on a boat—how they laughed at that one. I dock more quietly now, though never without a dose of trepidation.

The seasons came and went as I campaigned to excite my young crew with the joys of being a weekend sailor. While I was never able to light the flame of nautical passion in their hearts, it didn't prevent us from sharing a lot of laughs and adding to the trove of family memories—the good, the bad, and a few of the uglies.

There was the speech I delivered during the 3-hour drive to Maryland where I harped on the absolute importance of staying on the boat, as in not falling overboard. That little lecture was barely an hour old when I stepped from dock to deck, with both arms full of gear, just as a gust of wind pushed the boat to the ends of her dock lines. Stepping onto the thin air where the boat had so recently been, I went down so quickly I didn't even have time to yell before hitting the water. I swam the few yards to the boat's transom and hauled myself aboard in time to see the children's faces change from fear to laughter. It was another lesson learned and worth the wet clothes.

There was Freeway, the beagle pup I felt compelled to make a home for after Steven presented his list of ten reasons why we should get a dog. My favorite: "Said to be man's best friend." Freeway was no longer a puppy, but his maturity had not brought him any sea legs. On one memorable outing he vomited all over the cushions on one side of the cabin and then slept on the other side until he decided to hurl on those cushions also. Freeway was beached after that, and no doubt pleased with the outcome.

There was the afternoon sail where I grounded the boat just outside Rock Hall Harbor. Having missed the channel entrance, we were left with a beautiful view and a long wait for the tide to rise. It was a lovely night, mildly tempered by complaints that the only provisions on the boat were bread and cheese. We still refer to cheese sandwiches as boating food. But we had music and games and life without television.

And there will always be the hot July day on the Chesapeake with a whispering wind and no cloud cover. Amy still refers to that sail as the day I tried to kill them. Steven had been invited to spend the weekend with a friend, so I had an all-female crew, Amy and Barbara. Barbara was a new woman in my life, the first since Gail. These were the early days of my relationship with a woman who would become the second love of my life. We were not there yet, but I was thankful that my decision to buy a boat hadn't put her off. I have always admired courage in a person, and Barbara was brave enough to date a man with two preteens, not to mention going sailing with a novice. Barbara and Amy both had the look that said: do you really want to go out and motor around on this scorcher of a day when there's hardly wind enough to sail? Actually it was more than a look, as they both asked the question a couple of times. I preferred light winds at that stage of my sailing competence, and I didn't think we had driven such a long way to just hang around the marina, so I suggested we sail to the Annapolis Bridge and back, a short afternoon sail.

We made it to the bridge in short order and the sail back should have been an easy downwind run in very light winds, but I was in a daze. The time spent on the boat was so enjoyable to me that I failed to realize that the position of the bridge behind us was not changing. The power of the wind from behind was just enough to fill the sails and offset the power of the current running against us. We might as well have been anchored. I now know how it feels to be 5 minutes away from a mutiny. Amy had taken to lolling about the cockpit panting, in what I interpreted as another exaggerated bit of acting from my beautiful daughter with a bent toward the dramatic. Barbara was as red as a beet, from what combination of sun and anger I wasn't sure. I did know that it was time to fire up the engine and make the best time possible back to the dock. We enjoyed a sumptuous dinner at the Beowulf restaurant, and by the time dessert arrived I was more or less forgiven.

I'm blessed with vivid memories of the kids splashing in the marina's pool, their young and carefree bodies reveling in the sun, and later devouring hot dogs as mustard dripped on their shirts. They loved all the surrounding activities, but they didn't really love the sailing. Sailing with my children was a dream I had, but at the end of the day it was a swing and a miss. When I commissioned *Steadfast* for her first season, Amy was eleven and Steven thirteen, not too old to fall under sailing's spell, but it just didn't happen. It was disappointing, but I could hardly blame them, and by then I could hardly sell the boat. Shoulda perhaps, but didn't.

I like to think that besides all the laughs, my children learned something useful from their time on *Steadfast*, if nothing more than the fact that you can't learn to sail, or very much else in the world, if you're worried about embarrassing yourself. Steven once asked me, after I had been seasick on an early season sail, why I continued to sail when I got seasick. I asked Steven why he continued to skateboard despite the frequent demands it put on our first-aid kit, not to mention his parentally frightening visit to the emergency room. He just smiled. We do what we do.

The wind is starting to drop back into the 20s, a more comfortable range, and it will be time to shake out a reef soon. We're on course and the hours are rolling by. There is a lot to do when singlehanding, but there are also times when there is nothing to do, times to fly off with a book for a bit. I retire below, pull out my bag of beef jerky, and tuck in at the nav desk with *Lonesome Dove*, a cowboy book that transports me to the plains of Texas.

DAY 9
OBSESSION

*If a man is to be obsessed by something, I suppose a boat
is as good as anything, perhaps a bit better than most.*

—E. B. WHITE

I have a friend, a sailmaker with no shortage of experience on saltwater racecourses. Joe has what he calls Joe's Cascading Cluster of
Events Rule. We all know the concept: you get a call from an old
friend to get together for a drink and the next thing you know it's
three o'clock in the morning, the two of you have decided to go
into business together on a theme restaurant, and you can't remember where you left your car. Well, perhaps not, but events can take
on a life of their own and lead to quite the clusterfumble.

Very early this morning the wind died and the main was
slapping around and making a horrible noise. The headsail joined
the jam session until I rolled it up and went back to sleep for an
hour. When the wind crept back at first light it was obvious that
the spinnaker pole was needed to give a little stability to the rig
in the very light air and stop the genoa from collapsing, so I went
on deck to set the pole. The spinnaker pole can be set a few feet
off the deck, and it runs from the mast to a corner of the headsail,
where it holds it out rather like a tent pole. It was then that I
noticed a small problem with one of the mainsail cars. These are
clever little gizmos that attach the mainsail to the mast. Each car
is attached to a track on the mast, and linked with a swivel to a

plate fastened to the forward edge of the mainsail. The swivels allow the sail room to swing out from the fixed mast, and the cars eliminate most of the friction involved in raising or lowering the sail. They make life a little easier, but like everything else on a boat, they need to be kept under surveillance. An attachment screw was missing from one of the cars, no doubt a casualty of all the slapping around, and I could see another unit halfway up the sail with a screw backed halfway out. It seemed advisable to lower the main completely and check and tighten all the hardware, particularly as the wind was still so light. I dropped the main and enthusiastically dived into this project, so enthusiastically in fact that I didn't realize that the mainsail halyard, the line that pulls the sail up, had gotten wrapped around the spreaders at the top of the mast. Fortunately, I saw that problem before I tried to winch one of the spreaders off the mast, but freeing the halyard took a ridiculous amount of time.

With the morning rapidly running away from me, I proceed to set the spinnaker pole and pole out the genoa. This is a pretty straightforward job, but not one I can do quickly by myself, as I have a strong preference for not getting whacked in the head by the pole or whacking the boat with the pole and leaving a ding that I would be explaining down the road.

I am now sipping my morning tea in the early afternoon, and it's hard to take much satisfaction from today's work. The boat was essentially standing still half the morning, but now, before the last dregs of my tea go cold, the wind is piping up and we are back at it, in a groove and heading west. Sweet! "Better lucky than smart," as they say on Wall Street.

With the off-course alarm rendered mute by the instrument problem, Hydro needs to be watched closely so we don't go on some undesired detour. I've been exchanging e-mails with a technician ashore, and his belief is that one of the instruments has gone bad. The recommendation is to disconnect the instruments one by one; hopefully this trial-and-error approach will identify the culprit and allow the others to get back to work. I determine to mount a new attack on the problem. After making a cheese sandwich, that old boat food again, and a large cup of hot chocolate I reach for the tool bag, and the afternoon drifts away as I chase after electronic gremlins.

The job is awkward, with little slack in the wires and the boat bouncing along, but I stick with it. I remove the panel and the chartplotter at the nav station, gaining access to the wiring and the autopilot control unit. For the first time I notice that there is a small cover on the bottom of the brain unit. I unscrew this cover and make the embarrassing discovery that there are slots for specialized fuses. On inspection I find that one of these fuses has blown. One look at the blown fuse and I know that I have no such spare onboard, not surprising as I had no idea that the unit had fuses inside. What a lame excuse! I should have known, and that's all there is to it. Once again the sea finds any weak link in your preparation. I fashion a bypass fuse but the autopilot is still out of action, so it's on to the rewiring. The only results from the afternoon's efforts are two very sore arms and the loss of my boat-speed instrument. The one instrument that still worked has joined the disabled list. Who knows why? All I know is that I might as well have taken a nap.

I do still have the GPS feed to the radio, so if I look at my radio I can see my position. To know your exact position at sea, at any moment in time, is something that sailors of old would have killed for.

This morning I wrote a blog to the race website saying:

"So as I sit here contemplating the past three days . . . and thinking that we're into June and I'm still wearing long underwear and three layers of clothing and having hot oatmeal for breakfast, the thought occurs: what's wrong with this picture? Actually nothing, it's the OSTAR and I'm loving it."

But I'm not loving it now. I'm so demoralized that even a little James Taylor on the stereo doesn't change my mood from morose to mellow. All this screwing around with equipment issues—generator, autopilot, instruments—and I have simply not been sailing fast enough. I haven't gotten any feedback on my position relative to the fleet for a couple of days, but it has to be slipping and I can't blame *Rubicon*. She can be sailed fast and we started the race doing just that. I consider changing course for the

Azores. I would not be the first to retire from this race, number seven I think, and it is warm in the Azores, and they have some fine restaurants in Horta. I know because we stopped for a brief visit on the eastbound passage. I could then get the boat sorted out and be back in Newport for most of the season. If I am going to divert, now is the time to do it, while I can still lay a good course for the archipelago. I work out the course, write it down in my notebook, and spend a few long minutes staring at the figure before drawing a big X through it. I'm not the only one having equipment problems in this race. The destination is Newport, and the destination is more important than the arrival date.

These boats are wonderful and terrible things. They are thieves of the first order, taking you from your family, stealing time from worthy pursuits, and writing checks that mock your attempts at financial planning. These boats are thieves, but redemptive and generous ones. You must work for their gifts, but they will be your guide and sherpa to a world you cannot know without them. They will take you to the sea that you can never come to know from the deck of a cruise ship, any more than you can come to know America from driving the interstates.

Taking in the seascape from the deck of a cruise ship can indeed be breathtaking. Like standing atop a tall building, the elevation delivers a more distant horizon to your gaze. Looking down on the ocean from such a height provides a vast and constantly changing panorama, visited by every shade of blue, green, gray, black, and white, but never a shade of ugliness. You are, however, disconnected, and in the same way that a rooftop view disconnects you from life on the streets. There is also the temporariness of your engagement, as you return inside the bowels of the ship for meals, entertainment, and libations. On a sailboat, you're at sea level, and in anything but a flat calm you're at eye level. You feel the pulse of life on the ocean, recognizing the arrival of swells from a distant storm, watching a school of flying fish chased out of the water and finding one on your deck, and attracting dolphins to delight you while they inspect your boat. And there is nothing temporary about it. You are in the life until you bring your boat into port. I do not claim to know the sea, but I am making her acquaintance. There are clues out here for those who want to know this world, and who want to know themselves.

I have occasionally wondered what flight of madness possessed me to buy a sailboat, a step I took in middle age, a step that a financial advisor—if I had one—would no doubt have counseled against, and a step that my friends—the old nonsailing ones anyway, and that was all of them at the time—viewed with puzzlement, and that only when they were being kind. I had no time for a boat. At home, I felt surrounded by jobs that needed doing, reminding me daily of my neglect. At work, I wrestled a "to-do list" that pulsated, but never seemed to shrink. I was sure in the knowledge that those parenting years defined the word "precious," though it was a confused affair at times as I fumbled with the tools in the parental kit bag in various attempts to guide my young charges through their adolescence to the threshold of adulthood. In retrospect, a boat made no damn sense. I can only confess to an obsession. I could not get out of my head the siren song pulling me to visit this ocean in this way. Yet even on the boat tethered in a marina, I have always felt an affirmative shout from my soul. Yes, this boat will be a part of me and I a part of it, our destinies entwined.

There was a brief time when I thought it sounded vaguely incorrect—politically, that is—to refer to a boat as "she." Concerns about political correctness have never registered very high on my worry meter, but being thought a man of reactionary tendencies, one who didn't see the full and total emancipation of women in the world as the true blessing that it is—well, that was another matter. A little research gave me the crutch to address this most minor of dilemmas.

According to the traditionalist argument, the ancient naming of ships after goddesses and the carving of feminine forms as bowheads for ships gave rise to the view of ships as feminine. This was carried through the later centuries when ships were named after those lesser goddesses that are our significant others. I'd put my money on this explanation, though it provides no ammunition for the current debate.

Fortunately, the linguists have come to the rescue. While most of the grammatical gender has fallen away from modern English, the early roots of the English language, and the roots of Romance and indo-European languages generally, show that many nouns had grammatical gender, and were either masculine or feminine. Ships, by chance or design, were feminine. The linguistic explanation is logical and fact based, though it does beg the question of why gender remains attached to boats and ships while separating from the rest of the noun world.

Apparently *Lloyd's List*, the journalistic resource of the shipping industry, has already been referring to a ship as "it" for some time, but really, have you seen some of those ships? They're behemoths. Hugely impressive, efficient, and ugly. My research ended one afternoon when I was standing on the dock as a sailboat turned into the channel. I didn't have it in me to think of her as anything but a she.

If I'm ever called to task for referring to a boat as "she," I'm sure I'll trot out the linguistic argument. Of course, who would raise the objection but one blind to the beauty, form, and grace of a sailing vessel?

Whether it makes any sense to invest more time and effort in trying to resolve the electronics problems on *Rubicon* is no doubt a sensible question to ask myself at this point. Staying fast and on course is probably a wiser use of my energies. On the other hand, I've just tossed half my dinner overboard; it was seasoned with the sour taste of defeat. Wisely or not, I'll launch another attack on the problem, and hopefully no new issues will change the agenda.

We're riding smoothly with the full main and the poled-out headsail carrying us west-southwest, a fine course. A small sea is running. It's overcast again, of course.

ZEPHYRS

A sailor is an artist whose medium is the wind.
—WEBB CHILES

Today is a fine day at the office and after a quick breakfast I turn my energies to keeping the boat moving in very light air. We're still running with the full main and the poled-out genoa, and the sails look mighty pretty against a clearing sky. The sun is shining, the day is warming, and the seas are flat and comfortable; long may it last. Driving this marvelous machine and watching her cleave a path to Newport, there is no place that I would rather be.

As a racing sailor, light air is what you wish for your competitors, not for yourself, but times of light air will arrive and they should be embraced. Raging against fortune can be fun, even if it's not energy efficient, but the real reason to skip the rant is that you don't want to miss the beauty. With no need to hold on and brace your legs to avoid adding another bruise to your collection, you can relax and watch the miles slide by. You are not becalmed, you are not drifting; you are on a controlled course. Progress is measured, limited by current conditions. So be it. It is one of the most peaceful feelings in the world. Cruising sailors too often miss this experience when they have schedules to keep and succumb to the temptation to turn on the iron genny (the engine) as soon as their boat speed drops below some number they have fixed in their minds.

There are skills to be mastered with light-air sailing, just as there are with heavy-weather sailing. In heavy weather, you are trying to go as quickly as possible without putting undue stress on the rig, blowing out a sail, or doing the sailing equivalent of a spinout. In light-air sailing, you are trying to go as quickly as possible while staying motivated to work the boat and ignore the devil whispering in your ear that there is too little wind to sail, that you should stand down until conditions change. *Rubicon* is of moderate weight for her size and she can be quite fast, but she was designed as a performance cruiser, not a race boat. She is certainly faster with wind strength over 10 knots, but she will happily sail in less, and what a joy it is.

There is nothing that gives a sailor more satisfaction than stepping into the cockpit, adjusting a few lines, and seeing the boat accelerate, and there are so many strings to play with: sheets to position the sails, halyards to adjust the vertical tensions, traveler and vang lines to control the position of the boom. Light-air sailing requires monitoring, tweaking, and driving even as you soak in the peace of the day, but seeing the boat speed add a tenth of a knot brings a smile to my face, and half a knot is cause for celebration. Of course, *Rubicon's* boat speed indicator is not communicating at all today, just staring blankly from its assigned position in the row of dark instruments over the main hatch. Sensory perceptions must guide my judgment, just as they have coached sailors over the millennia.

It is always best to adjust one control line at a time, particularly when fine-tuning. If you make a number of changes at once, you can't trace the result to the cause. Many times the change will have a positive impact, but sometimes it will be neutral and, not so rarely, you will have overshot the mark and eased a line out too far or winched one in too tightly. As with doctors, the first principle is to do no harm.

On a fully crewed racing yacht, sail trimming is a constant operation as minor adjustments are made to catch each puff of wind, and sail changes can be slightly less prophylactic when fit and rested crew are always on deck. In the solo situation, time and energy are both rationed commodities, so there are fewer sail changes and less fine-tuning. Beyond those differences, sails remain the engine of the operation, as wind is the fuel, and after a stint of 24/7 days on the boat you will sense when that engine isn't fully with the program, and you will not be able to ignore the joyous labor of sail trim.

The report card on sail trim is boat speed, and so the boat-speed indicator becomes another obsession. I can now claim something in common with Sir Francis Chichester, the great circumnavigator and booster of solo sailing, who wrote of his emotional trajectory following the loss of his speed indicator. It may have been during his own OSTAR race, or one of his other passages, but I remember his account of how he raged in frustration at the breakage, and then the calmness that settled over him as he allowed his mind and gut, not the dictatorial speed monitor, to tell him when to be satisfied with his performance.

I've been asked how long it takes to learn to sail, and my usual response is to relate my experience in taking a one-weekend introduction-to-sailing course. You can indeed learn the basics in a "learn-to-sail weekend," but the answer I prefer is the one given by the old salts, who like to say, "the rest of your life." Certainly many things besides sailing can take the rest of your life to master, but I haven't heard the admission as often in other areas. Particularly in business, it is common for people to pretend that they've got all the factors nailed, and we can see where that mind-set has brought us. I cannot imagine reaching the point where I'm convinced that I have it all nailed, and I'm not at all sure that I would want to sail with someone who held that perspective. Most of the sailors I've met freely admit that they learn something new every day they spend on the water. To be sure, most of my sailing companions have been recreational sailors who, presumably, have more to learn. Professional sailors are a small occupational category, and I've yet to poll them, though their answers might not be so different. I worked in the investment business for almost thirty years and I learned something new on most days.

The one part of the process that I do think I nailed pretty well was choosing the name *Rubicon*. The naming of a boat is not something to be taken lightly. I kept the name *Steadfast* on my first boat, not because of the silly superstition about changing a boat's name, but because the name itself was a virtue, it was distinctive, and I admired the previous owner, who bought such a serious sailboat when he was seventy-five and sailed it until he was eighty. When I ordered *Rubicon* I suspected that she would be my last boat, and certainly my only new boat, so the naming decision was given appropriate thought.

Rubicon is the name of a river in northern Italy that, in ancient times, was an important boundary. When Julius Caesar took his army across that river in 49 BCE, he broke Roman law and ignited the civil war that, a few centurions later, established him as dictator of Rome. He is said to have uttered the words "the die is cast," possibly repeating a proverb of the time, "let the die be cast," as he mounted his horse and entered the river. I remember my father using the term "crossing the Rubicon." It's a phrase you don't hear much these days, but one that's come down through the years to define a decision or action that is both consequential and irrevocable. Caesar may have derailed Rome's early attempt at democracy when he became "dictator in perpetuity," but he did give us a great boat name. It struck me that the name might be ever so slightly grandiose, but to my ear it sounded lyrical; indeed, every bit as lovely as the boat, and so the name was settled.

It is odd that I did not have any major plans, let alone Rubicons to cross, when I ordered this beautiful boat and wrote that first check. It was a year before I would take delivery of *Rubicon*, and many months before the sale of the firm where I worked would be on my radar screen. Yet as events unfolded, she was commissioned the week I retired, and now we are in the middle of the Atlantic. Funny.

One more deck job to do today and that is to jibe the boat (turning the back of the boat through the wind), then reposition the sails on the opposite side. Sailing downwind, sailors usually jibe the boat to move the wind from one side of the boat to the other; sailing upwind, the typical maneuver is to tack the nose of the boat through the wind. This is usually a pretty straightforward exercise and involves trimming the mainsheet, which controls the mainsail, and the new jib sheet. I say new, because there are always two sheets attached to a headsail: the working sheet, which is the one in use

at any particular time, and the lazy sheet, which is on the opposite side of the boat. Whenever you tack or jibe the boat, the lazy sheet becomes the working sheet and vice versa. In any event, right now it is slightly more work than it would otherwise be because I have the genoa poled out on the spinnaker pole, meaning everything needs to be reset on the opposite side. Conditions are benign, and *Rubicon* is soon sorted out and trimmed for the new course.

It is staying light later as we sail west and as the season changes, and my dinner hour moves with it. I realize that today needs to be capped with a good dinner: nothing new has broken, it's warming up, and we're headed more or less to Newport. I'm pleased that an impulse prompted me to buy a couple of frozen pizzas before leaving Plymouth. The box says it serves two to three people, so it's a good thing I'm solo today because I'm eating the entire thing. I think that my sense of taste declines as the distance to the nearest restaurant increases, but the pizza is a treat and I eat it slowly while sipping a can of Coke and listening to some old Loggins and Messina tunes. The pizza is followed by a large square of chocolate. It may not be the recommended dinner of the American Heart Association, but after a glorious day of sailing, contentment is displacing the frustrations of yesterday.

BECALMED

Everything can be found at sea
according to the spirit of your quest.
—JOSEPH CONRAD

The peace of slow sailing came to an end late last night, and the intervening hours have been spent drifting in a spot of the ocean where there is either no wind or such light and shifty wind that it's impossible to step out in any direction. Whether from the irregular movement of the boat as it rocked in place, frustration over the lack of progress, or the noise of the mainsail flapping about, it was not a restful night. I begin the day with bleary eyes looking out on a parade of waves that have blown here from somewhere, but left the wind behind.

In an ocean race there will be competitors in places with better wind conditions, but you cannot dwell on that fact; you must simply plot your own strategy. Sailing in light air is peaceful and quiet. The boat is stable and there is tremendous satisfaction in working to capture the maximum speed possible. After that you can put on some music, flip open a book, or work on the to-do list—no shortage there at the moment.

To be becalmed is to take a forced pit stop. There is nothing you can do to squeeze out that extra increment of boat speed; it's just zero. So you sit. Music helps, particularly Mozart, and Gregorian chants can put you in a zone where you know that this is all part of the order of things, but for the last hour I've been listening to old Willie Nelson songs. His ballad "Funny How Time Slips Away" has taken on a whole new meaning. This OSTAR is not getting any easier!

Most sailors have little experience with being stranded on a windless ocean. Being reasonably intelligent people, they turn on the engine when the wind dies. Of course, the use of an engine for propulsion, as opposed to battery charging, is not allowed in the OSTAR, or any other ocean race. In professional events, the propellers may be locked or some other restriction may be employed to ensure compliance. In an amateur race, compliance operates through the honor system. It would certainly be possible for a competitor to put his engine in gear for an hour or two here or there, and gain some possibly significant edge, but I don't think this has ever been a real problem in the sport. It is hard for me to think of a less defensible crime than cheating in a sailboat race. It strikes me as pure stealing. No justifications could be offered—not help to your family, or your career, or whatever. In fact, the only reward for winning is a short moment in a very small spotlight, plus whatever personal meaning one attaches to the achievement. Tiny rewards, totally debased, in return for losing your integrity are a pretty lousy trade. And if someone would cheat in an amateur sailing event, where in life wouldn't they cheat? Fortunately, it's rarely a problem in these events, and I've never met a competitor who has ever worried about it as a factor in a race.

In any event, for someone not in a race, there is nothing wrong with firing up the engine, certainly nothing wrong with being a powerboat guy or gal. Sailors are always turning on their engines because they are going too slowly, or they need to make port before a storm—or before Happy Hour ends. They never really visit the world of the becalmed. They are missing something, but unlike the joys of light-air sailing, what they are missing is a lesson in patience.

There are a few sides of town in this world of the becalmed. If the absence of wind is matched by the absence of waves and sea action, then the ocean can appear as flat as the proverbial millpond. The frustration of no progress is almost matched by the beauty of the boat's repose, and you can do some housekeeping, catch up on chores, read, or get some sleep.

The nastier side of town is where the sea state is still lumpy from leftover seas, ocean currents, or who knows what. In this neighborhood, where the sails cannot catch even a hint of wind to drive the boat through unsettled waters, you can feel like Dorothy looking out her bedroom window while her house banks and twirls. But I exaggerate; let's say Dorothy's passage in slow motion. This is also the noisier side of town as the rocking boat emits a cacophony of creaks, groans, and clatters. Providing percussion is the rattle of the mainsail cars on their track as the big sail is tossed about. The *sturm und drang* of it leaves you convinced that something is about to break, and not just your nerves. Such is the case now. Wallowing in this sloppy sea, the mainsail slats back and forth, banging and clattering as it hints of breakage to come. I consider dropping it completely, but compromise by reducing the sail to fully reefed status. With some sail up, I'm more likely to recognize the first signs of a returning wind, so I tuck in the three reefs, pull the lines taut, and retreat to a book. I'm still reading *Lonesome Dove*, the cowboy saga. It's a fine read, and fun to escape from a place that is cold and wet to a place that is hot and dry.

There is also the dangerous side of town in the world of the becalmed. These are areas where tides or currents are driving your boat toward a lee shore. With no wind to carry her to safety and no haven to steer toward, it could be the final chapter for the boat, if not for you. We're a long way from any shores, but contemplating this third scenario renders my current situation far less objectionable.

Earlier in the week I had calculated that I would pass the halfway point tomorrow, which just happens to be my fifty-eighth birthday, and I had fully intended to slice into my fruitcake, as delicious a birthday cake as I could want. The slow march of the past couple of days means that unless the OSTAR Race Committee decides to move the finish line to the longitude of the Grand Banks, my celebration will be on hold.

Despite some disappointment, I'm not so troubled by my progress in the race. That is what it is, and will be what it will be. I'm doing all I can to move things along, which right now is nothing, so there is time to think, and let my thoughts drift with the boat.

■ ■ ■

Albert Einstein once observed that life is like riding a bicycle. To keep your balance you must keep moving. The great scientist was right about that, and of course he knew that movement is not always visible to the naked eye. To grow as human beings we need action, but we also need contemplation. Contemplation occurs inside the mind, so we can be anywhere, though becalmed in midocean seems perhaps one of the better anywheres for an inner voyage.

The American writer Orison Swett Marden wrote that "work, love and play are the great balance wheels of man's being." How rare is it for any of us when all three of these great wheels are achieving their target RPMs, no gears grinding as we power through our daily runs?

The work wheel is behind me, at least for a time. I have left the profession I loved, the investment management business, now tarnished by its association with abuses and stupidity on Wall Street. There are many different "Wall Streets," many heads on the hydra-headed financial services industry, and none of them carry much luster these days.

What of the love wheel? I have been fortunate there. I have two great children on whom to lavish parental love and reap the dividends, and I've had two romantic loves, two long-term relationships, or LTRs as they are described these days.

I enjoyed seventeen years of marriage with Gail, and when I say enjoyed I mean that they were the happiest years of my life. When one loses a spouse, there is, it seems to me, no point in dwelling on any of the inevitable difficulties that visit a marriage. In fact, everyone likes to pretend that it was a perfect union, and it's easy to go along with that. I'm sure that if I had died on that terrible September day instead of Gail, I would have remained in her memory as a kind and loving husband and father, and the various problems in our history would have faded away. So it has been in my version of history. This is not to say that we didn't have a good marriage. We did. It might not have been made in heaven, but we tried hard to make it on Earth and we succeeded. The right side of my brain believes that if Gail had not died we would still be married. The left side agrees.

I met Barbara about a year after Gail died, just as I waded into the world of dating. We have been a couple for a dozen years now, and living together for one and a half. It has been a difficult relationship to accelerate, and we have not always tried, but there has been love. There is also love between her and the children, which is a blessing.

The play wheel of course is spinning fast and furiously. It is a lot of work out here, but I cannot think of it as work. I'm not a professional mariner. This is play. For a long time I refused to think of it this way because I took it so seriously; a silly perspective, for play it is. It is recreation or, perhaps more properly, re-creation.

When I read Marden's comment I thought that he had forgotten the spiritual wheel. However godless or god fearing each of us may be, there is a spiritual component to our being. I realize now that spirituality is not Marden's forgotten wheel. It's the harmony that results when each wheel is turning in its proper manner and at its proper speed. Then a life is tuned, and in harmony with its time and place.

"Happiness is not a matter of intensity, but of balance, order, rhythm and harmony," wrote Thomas Merton. I think that is one of the seductions of life at sea, perhaps the primary one. All of those forces are here, and in abundance, but you must put yourself in sync with them. Nature will not synchronize to you.

I will have work to do ashore.

Just as I go below to record my noon position and prepare some lunch, the breeze returns, a curious but welcome bit of timing that is more than sufficient to delay a visit to the galley and get this show back on the road.

I trim the sails and soon we are sliding along at 6 knots or so in 3-foot seas. Now for that egg and cheese sandwich! Today's basket of e-mail brings notes of encouragement and early birthday greetings. It was a fine dessert. I am happy.

BETTER LUCKY THAN SMART

Wherever you go, go with all your heart.
—CONFUCIUS

Wakefulness is seeping in, but I remain stretched out on my sleeping mat. It has been a good sleep, or as good as they get in solo sailing. Alone on the boat I rarely sleep too soundly or too long. My sensors remain on in the background and a new sound, a change in the boat's movement or attitude, and I am awake. *Rubicon* is powering along and all seems well, but I'm suspicious of the course. Clouds cover the sky as they have more often than not since the starting gun was fired, so I have no visual clues from the sun, and without any instruments I cannot glance over to the nav station for a course update. I pull on my seaboots and go up to the wheel to check the binnacle compass. Sure enough, the wind has come around and we're well and truly off course. Damn! This is no way to run a race, but what can I do? The off-course alarm is tied to the electronic compass instrument and that's out of action. What will the people looking at the tracker think?

I have no idea how long we were romping off in the wrong direction, but we're back on course now and as I linger over my breakfast I know that I have little to complain about.

Today is my fifty-eighth birthday and I'm at latitude 46° N, longitude 28° W and change. *Rubicon* is moving well and in the right direction, and I wonder if the same is true for me. At sea we are a team, but after we tie up in Newport the team will part for a time. Birthdays are logical points for taking stock, and I certainly have the time and space for it out here. Perhaps if I do it now, it will be easier to just motor right past the sixty mark in two years.

I've been a bellyacher about many things over the years, but rarely about the loss of my youth. I survived my youth, and I wouldn't care to return to it. I have had a life to live and I have lived it, and for that I have computers and the United States Marine Corps to thank. I remember the moment when I could finally say, "Vietnam, come and gone."

It was July 1970 when I left Vietnam, transportation courtesy of the U.S. Navy. We left in the falling dusk, marines lining the rail as the twinkling lights of Da Nang and the lush hills embracing the city fell slowly over the horizon. My mood was a mix of gratitude and serenity, a lovely combination. I remember thinking that I should never worry too much about anything again. That mind-set was evaporating even before we docked in Hawaii. It could never survive the daily flow of life's tribulations, but few weeks go by when I don't say, "Peter, you're a lucky SOB. Be grateful." I think this may be a common feeling among veterans who have moved on with their lives, and know that the blood of better men remains in the zone they only visited. Carrying this sense of gratitude has been a gift that has helped me many times in my life. A gift from the war. It sounds strange, but very little about war is simple.

I had been stationed at the sprawling base outside the port city of Da Nang in what was then South Vietnam. It would be five more years before that bloodied land would lose the "North" and "South" from its name, and the long path toward viewing Vietnam as a country rather than a war would begin. I was lucky. I was not a grunt, but a computer operator, assigned to help run an IBM 360 computer as it sorted out the details of the war. I changed tape and disk drives and pressed a few buttons. The hours were long, and sometimes you appreciated the change of pace when you were assigned to a convoy run, but it was all easy duty. I returned home with all of my limbs and none of the traumas that might later germinate into PTSD (post-traumatic stress disorder).

I received that honorable discharge, raised my children, was blessed with love, and labored in an exciting field, and soon I will have completed a solo passage across the Atlantic. I have checked the boxes I most wanted to check. Besides the kids, I'm not sure how much of it passes the "so-what test," but it has been a trip.

Next fall will mark my fifth anniversary of retirement. We define ourselves by what we do. When we stop doing, we lose our self-definitions, and we wonder where we fit in the world. With two children still in high school, and finally the economic possibility to spend more time at home, leaving the work world was an easy decision. Being there is a large part of parenting. I would have been a fool to miss the opportunity, though I do admit to stealing a day here and there to hone my sailing skills, and those days certainly grew in number after the graduations.

My first real job at seventeen was as a U.S. marine, at a time when those in the military ranks were held in low esteem due to their unfortunate connection with a losing war. My last job was as a partner and COO of a small but sterling investment firm. The firm is still sterling, untarnished by the miscreants and misdeeds bedeviling the financial services industry in recent years. My retirement, just a few years before scoundrels of every stripe and from around the country dragged the repute of this very worthy field of human enterprise right into the mud, was pure luck.

I once read an anecdote about Winston Churchill's reaction after losing his last bid to be prime minister. His wife, attempting to console him, said that his loss was probably a blessing in disguise. His wonderful rejoinder was the observation that it was indeed a very effective disguise. That's how I've come to think about the loss of the boat instruments on *Rubicon*. There was a wealth of information in those numbers. Harvesting that data can be a great asset in racing efficiently, inputs to help you sail fast and smart. Now I feel like a financial analyst without any numbers to crunch, someone who can look only at the "story" of the company. How do you rate the stock then?

I've always admired those sailors who can sail a boat instinctively. Many of them honed their instincts at a very young age; indeed, many cannot even remember a time when they didn't know how to sail. Others who took up the calling later simply had that ability and developed those instincts as others might do with music or language. My progress from armchair sailor to blue-water sailor came later in life, and it quickly became clear to me that I was not an instinctive sailor, so I have learned by the book, trying to understand why *B* should happen if you do *A*, and under what conditions you should do *X* or *Y*. I even have a binder filled with notes on what I've learned about sailing over the years and how certain things need to be done on *Rubicon*. I review it in the spring to brush the cobwebs aside. Now the only instruments at the helm are the compass and my eyes and ears, so I have become ever more conscious of wind and sea conditions. Before I might have glanced at the instruments and thought, "OK, it's blowing 20 knots so my preferred sail combination is probably the solent headsail and one reef in the main." Now I look harder at the sea conditions, I hand steer for a while to get a sense if any weather helm has developed in the wheel, I glance more frequently at the telltales (little ribbons attached to the sails that show how the air is flowing by and from the sails), and I listen more closely to the boat.

Of course I want to get my instruments back one day, but this sailing has a certain charm. My eyes are fixed on the sea, the sky, and the set of the sails. Numbers may float in my mind, but the barrage from the instruments has ceased. It feels primal. It may take more than a transatlantic passage for me to become an instinctive sailor, and perhaps I never will, but the partnership between boat and skipper is closer now and the joy of sailing is making that partnership work.

SIGHTING A WHALE

It is a bad plan that admits of no modification.
—PUBLILIUS SYRUS

The wind fell below the sail point during the night, but it is quietly returning and finding its direction as I put water on to boil. As I start to focus, I realize that I'm not interested in breakfast if we can get moving again, so I turn the kettle back off, grab a handful of almonds, and head on deck. The wind has announced its direction and *Rubicon* is taking hers. We are in light air, which is a huge improvement over no air, and I spend the morning coaxing out the miles.

When I have done about all I can do to get the boat moving, my mind turns to food, but just as I turn my body to get by the wheel, I catch a glimpse of a dark bulge about a hundred yards off the starboard side of the boat. There's no time to retrieve the camera so I just absorb the moment. The bulge quickly disappears to be replaced by the long black body of a whale, and the next frames reveal the body slipping below the slate-gray surface and the tail climbing out of the sea to wave good-bye. It might have been a sperm whale but I can't be sure. My *Field Guide to North Atlantic Wildlife* has sections on all the whales and that's the only one that seems to match the color, size, and shape, and particularly the lack of a dorsal fin. The book says they can dive for up to an hour and they usually do the tail roll before a deep dive. Huge, majestic, and graceful, truly a sight to behold. If my autopilot had been working

I might well have missed seeing today's whale. Perhaps there's a whale every day. I stay on deck for a long time after that, but the whale has moved on.

I laugh as I remember my first thought when I saw the whale and how my mind had flashed to the location of the EPIRB, a remarkable device that can be set off in case of emergency and which, in probably less than 24 hours, would have a diverted ship converging on your position. It seemed clear to me that the whale, easily the size of *Rubicon*, could sink her if so inclined. Perhaps not without some injury to the whale, but that would be slim comfort. There have been documented cases of boats hitting whales, or vice versa. It is not always clear who violated the navigational rules, and of course only one version of these collisions is ever reported. I considered it likely that for every small-boat collision with a whale there were a thousand sightings, and it was with that conjured statistic in mind that I forgot the EPIRB and concentrated on the magnificence of the event.

We are sailing now with a real wind from the southeast, which is just fine for pointing *Rubicon* west. The winds will always set one-quarter of the horizon as a no-go zone for sailors, but that still leaves three-quarters of the compass directions open to travel. We each have our no-fly zones. In America we like to believe that people can be anything, do anything, and go anywhere. There are worse illusions to grow up with; in fact, I drilled these very notions into my own children. I still do when given the chance. Adults know that some roads are blocked, but fortunately they also know that many roads lead to Rome, or wherever. Thank God boats and people can tack, and there are few points that cannot be approached from the right angle.

Just before leaving for the OSTAR, I was watching the television news and heard a politician say that he never thinks about plan B because he considers it defeatist. Even by the rarefied standards of politicians, this was first-class bullshit. Most people my age have long since left plan B behind, let alone plan A, sometimes in sorrow, sometimes in joy. I was working on plan D by my twenties, and I'm well into the alphabet now.

■ ▪ ▪

The day I started high school I knew there was only one college I wished to attend, the U.S. Naval Academy at Annapolis. The military had been my career choice from a young age, a line of work where the appeal was honor and purpose more than glory. I think my father's generation set me up for it. All the fathers seemed to have served in the war. Those who have seen war will swear there's no glory in it, but there can be a purpose, a reason to fight the just war. The purpose seemed revealed to me at a young age, when I was just starting to read newspapers, and I read about the Eichmann trial.

Adolf Eichmann was the senior Nazi charged with formulating and overseeing the plans that led to the murder of virtually all of the European Jews. He was captured by the Israeli Mossad in Argentina in May 1960, then spirited back to Israel where he was put on trial in the spring of 1961, found guilty of crimes against humanity, and hung in 1962. He remains the only criminal ever executed by the state of Israel. It was big news when the Israelis captured him, though I don't remember it. It was bigger news when they put him on trial, and I do remember that, even though I was just turning ten. It seemed inconceivable to me that anyone could have committed the crimes he was charged with, so I read about the war and, though a difficult enterprise, it struck me as the marriage of noble purpose to high adventure. There was a map of the world in my tenth-grade history textbook, and every country was either red or black. The red countries were identified as "slave states." They were the communist countries, and it seemed there was work to do.

Unfortunately, I was barred entry into any of the military academies by a crisp governmental catch-22. The academies do not accept anyone who is not a U.S. citizen, which seems a reasonable requirement to me, though it blew my plan A out of the water. I had immigrated with my family when I was six and we were all British citizens. As a minor child, I could become a citizen only if my parents took that step first, and they were content with their green cards. I could become a citizen independently once I turned twenty-one, but you cannot apply to the service academies after the age of twenty and a half. That seemed like a tough nut to crack, and I never did, though I went halfway around the world before I gave up.

Eventually I developed what I thought was a very clever plan, my plan B. I would graduate from high school a year early, join the Marines, get my ticket punched in Vietnam, and apply to the Naval Academy after my valiant military service. It was not easy, particularly the pestering. I pestered my high school principal to allow me to graduate a year early. I pestered my parents to sign the permission slip I needed to join the Marine Corps as a seventeen-year-old, and when my orders for "The Nam," as we called it, were changed to Okinawa at the last minute, I pestered the gunnery sergeant of my company until I got my transfer to Vietnam.

My B plan bogged down in Vietnam. At least mine wasn't the only one. I was in Vietnam, but not in the war. After boot camp at Parris Island, South Carolina, the Marine Corps, without bothering to solicit my views, ordered me to report to the computer school in Quantico, Virginia. This was before PCs, when computers were monstrous machines but already indispensable. The result of that education was that I worked in a large air-conditioned bunker while my helmet, flak jacket, and rifle hung by the door, clean and unused. No guns, no glory.

I considered pestering once again, and this time for a transfer to the infantry, to the grunts. Our base in Da Nang was too strong to invite an attack from the NVA (North Vietnamese Army), let alone the VC (Viet Cong), but the grunts knew how to find the war. They found it on long-range patrols where they sought out the enemy and vice versa, and they came back when they were done, or short of ammunition, or had simply called in so many medevac choppers that it was time to limp home.

I was thinking about all of this one evening when I went to the outside movie at our base in Da Nang. It was starting to rain so I wore my helmet and poncho, and the movie was *Patton*, where George C. Scott plays the great American battlefield general of WWII. All the benches were taken, so I was one of a small group standing in the rain watching Patton's Third Army roll across Europe, with occasional interruptions from our own war. About halfway through the movie, the ships offshore started their nightly shelling. It sounded, as it always did, like a low rolling thunder as the big shells were sent on their singular journeys. A short while later some flares started floating down outside our perimeter, no doubt a precaution launched by a jumpy guard. The marines watching the movie paid no attention; they were not interested in our war. The one on the big screen—or in this case, a big sheet—was more interesting to them and more satisfying. That was the good war, the "Crusade in Europe" as Eisenhower had called it.

I've often thought that computers saved my life, but it was the grunts, too. I knew many of them. The zeitgeist in the Marine Corps was that we were fighting the last phase of a losing war, which turned out to be true. The marines and soldiers continued to do everything that was asked of them, but morale was infected. Troop levels were already being drawn down when I arrived, and perhaps that raised the spirits of some, but as memory serves it was never viewed as a sign of success. The tide had turned against us, there was no talk of victory, and we knew we would not be going home to any parades. It was simply a holding operation. Well, not "simply" at all actually, but it was a holding action. Even Walter Cronkite, the voice of journalistic authority, had come out against the war by then.

Discretion finally got the better part of whatever valor I may have had, as I absorbed the reality that if you go on enough patrols your luck will run out. Sniper, ambush, or booby trap, the enemy had many cards to play. This was not *Sands of Iwo Jima* with John Wayne. Nerve aside, the whole plan seemed to have lost its point. I stopped pestering, did my job, and grew to accept the knowledge that others had done the heavy lifting. The things we have to live with, and if we live, the things we live for, are what make a life.

The wearing of the uniform had lost its appeal, though I would grow proud of my service as the years went by. All I received were the show-up medals, and I never applied to the Naval Academy. The GI Bill offered one month of college support for each month of service, so after three years in the corps I had my four academic years covered. I was off to college, starting September classes one week after my discharge. I was on to plan C.

For years after my discharge I read wide and deep on Vietnam. I needed to understand what went wrong, and why so many people (Vietnamese, Cambodian, Laotian, French, and American) died over so many years for so little improvement in the human condition, in Southeast Asia or anywhere else. It was hard to pin down when things really went wrong. The only thing that seemed clear was that you couldn't blame that one on the oil companies. Many people blamed Johnson for the buildup, or Kennedy for his earlier decision to send military advisors. To blame any one person, or even a few, for that multigenerational fuck-up seems rather ridiculous, but it was and remains common practice, so at the end of the exercise I decided to pin it on Truman. Harry Truman was an admirable president in many ways, but I suspect he could have written all he knew about Indochina on the back of a postcard.

As the Second World War came to a close Harry instructed his emissaries to snub Ho Chi Minh, who had waged a guerilla war against the Japanese. Ho wanted independence for his country and desperately wanted U.S. support, in no small part as a bulwark against China, Vietnam's historic enemy. He even used an entire section of the U.S. Declaration of Independence in the speech he made announcing Vietnamese independence in September 1945. It was a busy day in history, as it was the same day that the Japanese signed their surrender documents on the battleship *Missouri*. You have to wonder how history would have played out if we had held out the hand of friendship to Ho as the Japanese army was going home. Perhaps there would have been no killing fields there. Instead, unfortunately, we did not just snub Ho, but used the U.S. Navy to clear Haiphong harbor of mines and loaned American ships and landing craft to the French to facilitate the return of their colonial army of occupation. Harry didn't understand that colonialism was yesterday's news. Vietnam became a country it didn't want to become, and didn't have to become, and the window closed for rapprochement. So I took two lessons from Vietnam: we should be slow to reject would-be friends lest we make unnecessary enemies of them, and certain things, such as a navy, really should not be loaned out without a lot of consideration. It was the strategic blunder of our entrance that doomed us, not any tactical mistakes by the military.

The winds have built steadily throughout the day, and quite rapidly since lunch. The day that began with the mainsail fully reefed to limit the clattering as we rocked on the windless ocean is now ending with the main fully reefed because the wind is blowing over 30 knots and we don't want to catch any more wind, thank you very much. I have spent the afternoon hand steering downwind in the big breeze. Hydro could have handled it, but this was more exhilarating, a real hoot.

My shoulders are aching from the hours standing with one arm to each shoulder of the wheel's 48-inch circumference. I engage Hydro and go below where I put on a Charlie Parker CD and heat a dish of sweet-and-sour chicken. Served hot over rice, it is a challenge to eat slowly, and I savor it with a can of lemonade before the evening routine: the log, e-mails, a study of the weather charts, and my sea berth.

GREMLINS
FIGHT BACK

*The difference between
genius and stupidity is that
genius has its limits.*
—ANONYMOUS

A gale is expected over the next few days and I'm going through
the boat inspecting, securing, and generally getting ready for
the big blow. Despite the news packed in the weather maps,
the morning sky is clear and we're down to one reef. The sailing is
fantastic.

There are three parts to most offshore passages: the first few
days when you regain your sea legs and get into passage mode, the
last couple of days when you study the coast and harbor charts and
give the boat a good tidy-up, and the great middle where you are in
the rhythm of eat, sleep, sail. A passage to Bermuda, the classic blue-
water sail for East Coast sailors, is a grand experience but too short
to have much of a middle. On a transatlantic, most of the passage is
the middle. During the middle passage you are no longer working
to conform yourself to the new environment; you become one with
the boat and, apart from logging the noon position and updating
your ETA, you do not think much about arriving, just traveling
through. At fifty-eight, I still consider myself in middle passage and
I wonder how far I'll be able to extend the middle. This, however, is
a race, not simply a passage, so a little extra preoccupation with the

arrival date is allowed. My calculations allow me to still believe—hope, anyway—that I can finish in twenty-five days or less, though I will have to step up the pace a bit to accomplish that. *Rubicon* and I seem to be in a groove now. Perhaps all the equipment problems were packed into the first half of this race; then the second half could be a very different affair. Or not.

After a quick breakfast and tea my first task is to replace and reroute the control line for Hydro. This line has become frayed, but I change the lead of the new line so that it "runs fair" as sailors say, and this should eliminate a lot of the friction. It looks set to carry us to Newport.

With the minor accomplishment of restoring Hydro to good form, I consider a renewed attack on the instrument problem. Due to accessibility issues, and a very real desire not to disturb those items that still work (radio, GPS, AIS), troubleshooting has been a very slow process. The snail's pace of the investigation would not be so discouraging if there were a scintilla of progress to show for it. There is none, and I am totally lacking in any enthusiasm to tackle this job again. Maintaining the boat over the years has boosted my technical skills, but electrical work is not my strong suit at the best of times and now, alone and bouncing around in midocean, I can think of a hundred other ways I would rather spend the afternoon. I brew some coffee and listen to a Bob Seger CD. The thumping music soon energizes me and I roll up my sleeves, unscrew the access panel, and get to work.

Following the e-mailed suggestion from a technician, I'm going to rewire the SeaTalk bus, which controls the various instruments. We are sailing close-hauled, meaning that the boat is facing as close to the direction of the wind as possible without stalling out, and this "point of sail" leaves the boat heeled sharply. With the constant necessity to brace myself it's cramped and tedious work, and it consumes the afternoon. Finally the job is done, and despite my skepticism I feel a certain satisfaction in completing the task as I flip the instrument switches on the control panel and hop on deck to check the status. Strike out! Not only are my instruments still dormant, but smoke is billowing from behind the control panel. This is certainly not the result I was looking for! It's also a major violation of the "no fire on the boat" commandment, and immediately increases my heart rate. Fire on a boat can quickly grow out of control, and taking to the life raft would be a grim proposition.

I immediately flip the main battery switches to the off position and reach for a fire extinguisher, but there is no need to pull the trigger. I watch and wait, but the burning is done. The fire in the wiring is out, the music is off, and my sigh of relief is soon replaced by a rant of sailorly swearing as I proceed to isolate the offending components. There is no further drama when I turn the batteries back on, but one thing is certain. The next time I tackle this problem will be in Newport; for now I will concentrate on sailing the boat.

I can't help feeling that Dad would be disappointed with the quality of my work on the boat today. Dad was an electrical engineer, a "double E" as other engineers refer to them, and no doubt a good one, as he stayed with it until retirement. He was Bernard James, but always went by Jim, and he was born in 1921 in the industrial city of Birmingham in the north of England. He was a good man, but always wore two chips on his shoulders, which is at least one chip too many. Perhaps that explained why he was volatile and scary, or perhaps it was in his genes.

He had been trained by British GE in the firm's apprenticeship program. Whatever the merits of this approach to learning the craft, it did not leave him with a college degree. In the 1950s, a bachelor's degree was not the necessary prerequisite for a professional job that it is today, though its absence was already unusual in an engineer. Dad felt that it held him back, a fact I learned from Mom. I think he felt some vindication the day he came home with a copy of a patent certification with his name on it, and of course the name of his company that was the economic owner of the achievement, but that was late in his career.

Dad's other resentment was the army, which had taken seven years of his life more or less involuntarily. Only many years later was soldiering a common bond between us. In my youth it was a point of conflict, as I wanted to be a soldier from about the age of ten and Dad had never wanted any part of it, or almost never. Dad's boyhood friend, also a Jim, had convinced him that they should both join the Territorials. The British Territorials were similar to the U.S. National Guard. The pitch was that joining up would get them out of their parents' homes for the occasional weekend, put a few pounds in their pockets, and give them uniforms, which might help in the perennial quest of young males for young females. I can only assume that the lads were not news junkies, or they might have questioned their timing. As it was, they were just in time to be mobilized after the Munich Crisis of 1938, when the fiction that another world war could be averted was stripped away. My father was just seventeen and he was in for the duration, one year until hostilities commenced and six long years thereafter.

My father was lucky, and it was a mystery to me that he never seemed to recognize it, but of course I had no standing to make that observation. Dad was wounded early on, shrapnel to the neck, and was recovering in a hospital outside London while the battle for France raged. After his recuperation, Dad was sent to Iceland, where he served in a radar unit. Despite its strategic location, Iceland was never invaded and Dad was not required to give any more blood for the cause. However he was separated from his friend Jim, who stayed in the battle. That was the first battle for France, the losing one. In less than two months, the Germans destroyed the French army and drove the British Expeditionary Force to the English Channel, where they were either captured or escaped at Dunkirk. Jim was captured and spent the rest of the war in a POW camp. He was riddled with tuberculosis at the time of his liberation, but eventually recovered. I met him when I was fourteen, when my parents broke the bank for a three-week vacation to England, where we reconnected with our extended family. I thought at the time that I was meeting the only real friend my father ever had. Dad is gone now, but he wasn't a sociable type and Jim might have been it.

Dad resented the big slice taken out of his life, and he vocally resented what he perceived as the attitude of the Americans that they had won the war. He called them Johnny-come-latelies, an old term for late arrivers. When I was growing up, everyone's father had been in the war; perhaps not for seven years, but time is only one dimension. The British held the standard for almost two years before the Russians came in, and almost two and a half years before the Americans joined the fight, but somehow my father seemed to take it personally. He did mellow as time went by, and I knew it was an act of forgiveness when in the late sixties he bought a Volkswagen, and a few years later parked a Toyota in the driveway. I've heard it said that to understand everything is to forgive everything, but there is a critical gap between when you understand and when you're prepared to forgive, and an even bigger gap when you never understand at all.

I think I've forgiven Dad for scaring the life out of me so many times when he would end an argument with my mother with the words, "I'm packing my bags and leaving in the morning." Single moms no doubt existed then, but the term had not yet entered the vernacular, and I would not have believed it possible. With no relatives in the country, I assumed that we would all be packed off to an orphanage. It terrified me. "Fool me once, shame on you; fool me twice, shame on me," as they say. Perhaps he believed what he said in the moment, but I was fooled for years as I operated on the assumption that our family was on the cusp of disintegration.

I'm feeling a little glum right now, having wallowed in these thoughts since the latest setback. The wind has dropped—the calm before the storm? Thickening clouds are covering the sky and I can still smell the burned wiring below. Pasta strikes me as the obvious remedy, and I boil up a huge pot of spaghetti. Ella Fitzgerald is singing "Blue Moon," about missing dreams and lost love. I slowly stuff myself while Ella pulls me out of my funk.

MOMENTS TO
REMEMBER

We are all in the same boat in a stormy sea,
and we owe each other a terrible loyalty.

—G. K. CHESTERTON

had a dream last night that I was driving home and was stopped at a police roadblock. The officer explained that I was about to enter a very bad neighborhood and I should turn around. "But officer, I live in that neighborhood," I said. After showing some identification, I was allowed to proceed and drive home, where I immediately bolted the doors and, for reasons that never escaped the obscurity of the dream, I found myself dialing 9-1-1. Not a comforting dream to have with a gale bearing down.

There are neighborhoods in the ocean. Some are friendly and welcoming, and you leave knowing you will count yourself lucky to visit them again. In others, once is enough, but you know that with a bit of bad luck, a glitch in your navigation, or a misreading of the weather—the master planner of neighborhood development at sea—you will be there again, perhaps in the dark of night whispering promises of better behavior in the future. Heartfelt commitments offered in trade for a safe passage.

Last night was not a restful one. Even before my dream of going home to a violent neighborhood, it was cluttered with interruptions that are now turning into those moments to remember at sea. About two in the morning I woke to the sound

85

of the high-water alarm wailing away not a foot from my ear. I was sleeping on my mat on the floor of the main cabin, still dressed in my foul-weather gear and boots. We were sailing close-hauled in weather that could already be called heavy, and some water will always find its way into the bilges under those conditions, water that is easily removed by the bilge pump. The heeling of the boat had simply caused enough bilge water to pool around the alarm actuator to sound the alarm. There are many alarms on the boat, but the high-water alarm is not one you want to hear in the middle of the night. I think I'll be remounting the alarm actuator a few inches higher in the bilge.

Sleep was just returning after the alarm episode when I was startled awake by a loud crash. One of the heavy ceramic coffee cups, which had been swinging happily on its hook since leaving Rhode Island in late April, had flown off and crash landed on the galley counter. The sound of ceramic meeting Corian screamed breakage. It was good to find that I'd lost only a coffee cup.

As I sit here listening to the soft howl of the wind, it occurs to me that there are many moments to remember in sailing, and thankfully, most of them don't even register on the worry meter. Those moments have framed my education as a sailor, and I think of an earlier time when I was stretching the envelope for this type of sailing.

I was standing on the deck of *Rubicon*, surveying the harbor at Vineyard Haven, the northern cusp of the jewel that is Martha's Vineyard. It was raining, lightly but steadily, and despite completing my pre-departure checklist, *Rubicon* was still firmly tethered to the mooring ball, safe and secure, as I watched the September gale snorting outside the harbor. I felt as I did on those occasional days in the business world when I woke feeling under the weather and not really up to the commute and a day in the office. My routine would always be to shower, shave, don my suit and tie, and then make the decision whether to head to the office. This approach prevented inertia from exerting too full a sway on the decision, and I generally headed out the door. That day, however, there was no suit and tie; instead I wore my Musto bib overalls, my Henri Lloyd offshore jacket with hood, and my Sperry seaboots. I was healthy enough, but I felt trepidation at the prospect of heading out in that weather and a strong desire to go below, where it was warm and inviting. I could make some hot tea, throw a couple of scones in the oven for a few minutes, and relax with a good book. That old sailor's expression rattled in my mind: "It's better to be sitting here wishing you were out there, than out there wishing you were sitting here."

It had been a fine week on the Vineyard, a location I fell in love with the first time I visited. I had returned to absorb its beauty, and to visit my friend David, a wise man who always helps me in my quest to understand the real mysteries of life: women. But that is another story. The NOAA radio bulletin had just announced that a gale warning was in effect with sustained winds out of the east of 25 to 35 knots, with gusts up to 40 knots expected. The forecast also specified visibility of 1 to 3 miles with patchy fog and rain, often heavy. I had been out in such weather before, but generally not when singlehanding and not in coastal waters. When you are well offshore and heavy weather hits, that is the one thing you concentrate on. In coastal sailing, regardless of the weather, many things demand your attention—navigation, traffic, shallows, etc. My plan was to sail to Newport, which should be an easy 6- to 7-hour sail, but as I felt the boat heel slightly I remained undecided. The mooring was behind the breakwater and the water was fairly calm; the heeling came from the wind hitting the mast, which rose well above the seawall. It struck me that this would be a great day to hank on the storm sails, but they now sat useless in my garage. I had taken them off the boat earlier in the summer when I was cruising with friends and wanted to free up some storage space. Oh well, I reasoned, a deeply reefed main and a token jib should fit the bill.

The minutes ticked by. As I looked over the seawall I considered that I have generally viewed prudence as a cornerstone of seamanship, and it seemed to be a cuspy decision. I decided to call Bill. Weather analysis is one of his strong suits. In fact, I met Bill while taking his "Weather for Sailors" seminar. Bill offered to check some weather sites on the Internet and call me back. I puttered about the boat for 20 minutes before my cell phone rang. Bill, adding enough color to the situation to help me reach my decision, said, "Stay conservatively canvased as there are some big cloud formations out there and they can hold powerful winds. If the fog closes in, have the engine on or ready to go." No sailboat can sail directly into the wind, and if that should be the direction you need to go in order to avoid some boat emerging out of the fog, you don't want any delays. He also observed that "there will probably be relatively little traffic out there, as most people who have a choice will be sane enough to stay in port." My passage would be mostly downwind, which should make for a calmer ride. It promised to be wet and uncomfortable, but I had a strong boat and sufficient experience. What we both understood was that you can't learn if you don't push the envelope, and it was for me to decide whether this was a good time for some stretching exercises. I thanked Bill and said I would call him from Newport.

I gave a little forward throttle to take the strain off the mooring lines, ran up to the front of the boat, lifted off the lines, and we were free. I then hustled back to the wheel and jammed the throttle forward to get the boat moving. A boat has no steerage until water is flowing past the rudder, so it's important to get underway quickly to overcome any wind or current on the boat, and avoid smacking any other boats as you leave the harbor. I was on the outside of the seawall in short order and motoring out of the harbor. I fell in behind the ferry leaving Martha's Vineyard and thought of the passengers sitting in the warmth with coffee and a newspaper. No matter, I was underway and where I wanted to be. About halfway out of the harbor I turned *Rubicon* into the wind, raised the mainsail, and tied in a couple of reefs. I then killed the engine and let *Rubicon* bear off to catch the wind. We were well and truly off, cracking along on a beam reach. As we passed West Chop and entered Vineyard Sound I turned the corner, bringing us further downwind and farther west. We swung over to port tack and I set the preventer, a piece of line that secures the boom and prevents an accidental jibe if a steering error should allow the wind to slip to the opposite side of the big sail, thus preventing the boom from blasting across the cockpit and delivering a possibly fatal head injury; a very useful piece of kit. I then unrolled about a third of the jib and settled in to enjoy the ride.

The wind was blowing in the mid-20s, more than enough breeze to keep *Rubicon* moving well, but less than I had expected. A commercial fishing boat appeared and was slowly passing about half a mile to port. There is one thing more fun than sailing, and that is sailing fast. My trepidation was gone. I was smiling broadly and tempted to shake out one of the reefs to give the boat a little giddyup. I thought that with a little more sail area we could stay ahead of the fishing boat that didn't yet know of my intention to race. Fortunately, I remembered the point about conservatism, relaxed a little, and left the reefs in place. Thirty minutes passed and the wind rose to the mid-30-knot range, where it stayed for most of the passage. By then we were cranking along at a fine turn of speed, and the waves were running, giving the boat plenty of movement as they rolled under the hull. Downwind sailing can be a roly-poly affair as the boat rides up and down as well as side to side. I was wearing my harness and clipped onto a strong point, but there are not many soft spots on deck or in the cockpit, so I kept a firm hold.

I stood at my station under the dodger where I could avoid most of the rain and worked my way through a block of Jarlsberg cheese and some bread as we rode over the slabs of gray water. The fog curtain closed in, and not wanting to experience any unexpected encounters of the nautical kind, I switched on the radar. I don't like sailing in the fog, and the heavier it is the less I like it. It's a little like crossing a minefield—you may do it successfully many times, but don't kid yourself that you've learned much from the experience, or that it will help you succeed the next time.

Finally the wind fell back to the mid-20-knot range. That 10-knot moderation soon brought us to quieter and more genteel surroundings. The rain was still falling, but it was a light spitting and visibility was returning. It was finally time to jibe around, put the boat on starboard tack, and head toward the buoy outside of Newport Harbor. After another hour, we passed Castle Hill and moved into protected waters. Once again I turned into the wind and the sails were soon dropped and secured.

Motoring into the inner harbor we soon found our way to *Rubicon*'s summer mooring. I made a last turn into the wind as we approached the mooring and ran forward to grab the pickup stick and haul the heavy mooring line onboard. Unfortunately, I approached a little too quickly and ran past the mooring line. *Rubicon* stopped, but without the critical mooring line attached she began to swing. It ain't over till it's over! I tore back to the wheel, jammed the throttle forward and guided her out of harm's way. Once more we came around and lined up the mooring ball. With a more measured approach, the run to the front of the boat proved successful. We were on. I secured the mooring pendants and wrapped the safety line around the cleats.

The passage was over, boat and crew secure. I was tired and wet and pleased. I had sailed cautiously and arrived safely. I called Bill to report a safe passage and thank him for the weather discussion. I knew I could walk into half the bars in Newport and find sailors who could have done that passage with ease, but all the same, my count of boats underway that day only came to three—or four counting the good ship *Rubicon*. As I contemplated the dinner specials at Crowley's Pub and sipped a well-earned glass of scotch, I realized that the only part of the day's passage that had frightened me was the decision to leave a snug harbor. All the "what-ifs" had bubbled up in my mind. Most were valid considerations, worthy of reflection, but the hardest ones, the ones requiring rejections were: What if I just stay home? What if I don't dare? I had stretched the envelope without shredding it, and so I counted it as one more step in my growth as a sailor.

Bigger waves are starting to join the party. The heavy weather is arriving, but I have a well-stocked library, music to play, and I know where I am; sailors of old could not even dream of this kind of passage.

The wind is now coming from west-southwest, so once again I am forced to choose a side. I'm taking the northerly side, hopefully a better route through the approaching weather front, and the winds behind the front should be from the north or northwest, which will allow us to sail a straighter course to Newport.

HEAVY WEATHER

He that leaveth nothing to chance will do
few things ill, but he will do very few things.
—MARQUIS (GEORGE SAVILE) OF HALIFAX

Rubicon is still wearing her heavy-weather wardrobe, the storm jib and triple-reefed main. We're still sailing close-hauled, and running in 9- to 12-foot seas. The spume being blown off their crests lends a dramatic and rather beautiful aspect to the blue-gray hills that are rolling by.

Bill, one of our band of three on the eastbound passage, is a professional sailor as well as a friend. With multiple transatlantic passages to his credit, he has learned a few things about passage-making. I was glad to have him on the boat going to England, and more confident of getting to Plymouth in good order. Bill and I are the same age, and we share the bond of being ex-marines, though it is a more believable fact with Bill, who still looks the part: tall, fit, and clean shaven with close-cropped hair. I never really looked the part, though I could at least describe myself as wiry in those years.

I've noticed that Marine Corps veterans generally wear their ex-marineness with a fierce loyalty, which may be very private or quite public. Some even reject the label of ex-marine, saying, "once a marine, always a marine." You're called many names in Marine Corps boot camp, but not till graduation day are you called a marine. It is a bonding experience. It was for me, anyway. I'm OK with the "ex," but I remain grateful for the lessons I received during my years in the Corps. They have stayed with me, and I suppose with more than a few others, as the Marine Corps' battle for the rear windows and bumpers of American cars must be included among its many victories. Despite being the smallest branch of the military, its decals dominate the landscape where Americans display their public affections.

Bill remembered his years in uniform vividly, and at times his presentation struck me as a quirky manifestation of his days in the Corps. He had no braggadocio about him, but there was a certain warrior spirit, which he generally wore lightly. Sometimes on patrol, such as doing deck work at the bow, he would point to an incoming wave and say, "Those waves are your enemies. They're out to kill you." He would also say that about a flogging sail, the boom, and occasional other pieces of gear. At first I was bemused, as I had never thought of the sea as my enemy. Had anyone asked, I would have replied that I loved the sea! Inexorably, as the miles and the weather systems rolled by, I became a convert to Bill's approach. It may be wise to think of these things as your enemies, particularly when far from any port. They may not be plotting to get you, but when they reach for you, it's best to be prepared.

I've stopped wearing a hat or a hood when I'm on the foredeck. This new practice gives me a better sense of what's going on, and lets me keep an ear out for any incoming waves. I listen closely for the one that wants to take me somewhere for a conversation I don't want to have. For some reason those waves seem to appear just as you're finishing up a job, and while you're still relatively dry. I heard the one last night just in time to duck and hold on for a quick drenching. Perhaps it was just as well; my hair hadn't had a wash since Plymouth.

I have been thinking a lot about fear lately, no doubt prompted by the rough weather *Rubicon* and I have been splashing our way through. This may not be the worst weather I've ever sailed in, but it's close, and it is the worst weather I've seen while alone and hundreds of miles offshore. It's odd that three things happen when darkness arrives on a stormy sea: the waves grow taller, the wind increases, and the shrieking of the wind through the rigging starts to sound personal. These verities, more nautical facts than meteorological ones, are even more pronounced when you are alone on the boat.

There are of course real considerations worthy of fear in this environment. The OSTAR has built a solid safety record over the years, and I don't believe there have been any fatalities since 1976, when that race, ravaged by storms, saw two sailors lose their lives. One was an American sailor, Mike Flanagan, who was washed overboard. The other was Mike McMullen, whose story is the most unfortunate chapter in the history of the race. His wife was accidentally electrocuted during the final days before the start as they worked to get the boat ready. Despite his grief, or perhaps because of it, he went ahead with the race and crossed the start line with the fleet. He told his friends and supporters that his wife "would have wanted him to do the race." He was never seen again, lost with his boat to storm, iceberg, or despair.

I tend to think of fear as a number on a scale of zero to ten, with zero being when you're home watching TV with your feet up, and ten when you've got some maniac pointing a gun at your head, or when you receive a note from the IRS saying they'd like to review your tax returns. Fortunately, there have been no high-end readings on this OSTAR, at least not yet, but the needle has bounced around a bit. Wind and waves have not caused the most anxiety, perhaps because there was some equally tough weather during the passage to Plymouth, and I know that *Rubicon* is one strong boat.

The fears that have started to multiply have less to do with conditions outside the boat than with those in my head. What if I don't do well? What will my friends and supporters think? What will my friends at Outbound Yachts think if I come trailing in late? They know their boat could be a class contender. What if I don't get to Newport in time to qualify as a finisher? An unlikely possibility perhaps, but this race has been filled with unlikely realities. These fears then yield a second generation that include: fear that I am being too wimpy and not pushing the boat hard enough (such as the time when conditions were abating and I could have taken the storm jib down but wanted no part of foredeck work while there was still drama at the pointy end of the boat), and even fear that I am using equipment problems or adverse winds to justify not staying in race mode.

Fears are like cockroaches; they can multiply at an alarming rate and before you know it, they are populating your life. So I have done a little spring cleaning and tossed all of these thoughts overboard. At the end of the day, the OSTAR is not a forum for whiners. It is an opportunity for a grand adventure where the challenges must be shouldered for the dividends to flow. Each race evolves as chance and circumstance deal out new cards, and every skipper has to play the hand that is dealt. My hand is fine.

Here's a heavy-weather sailing tip you won't read about in the sailing magazines: do the washing-up before it gets dark! The sounds of dishes clattering around in the sink as the darkened boat pounds off the top of waves will make you think you're in a Force 10 storm, even if it's blowing only 25 knots. It's best to keep the boat as quiet as possible.

Rubicon is barging her way through the gale. She's still pointing close to the wind and doesn't seem to need much attention from me today. I spend the day popping on deck like a jack-in-the-box, checking to see if anything is amiss or if any lines need tweaking, but she's rigged for the conditions and seems quite happy. That's just as well as I'm far more comfortable tucked into the bench behind the nav desk with a book. By the end of the day I've finished *Lonesome Dove*. It was a page-turner, all nine hundred pages of it, and I guess I'm in the right place for one of those. Of all the hundreds of details required to make ready for these back-to-back passages, one particular joy was selecting the basket of books to bring for two months at sea. I brought some serious books that have been on my list for a while, but right now I don't have the energy to wrap my mind around any of them. I just want some entertaining characters who will take me off the boat for a bit.

ORIGINS OF A RACE

> One of the tests of a good idea is its
> ability to last through the hangover.
>
> —JIMMY BRESLIN

It's not too uncomfortable below, as long as you have yourself braced or you're clutching a handhold, but it is a bit of a wild affair outside, and outside is never far away. Last night was as rough as I've seen it on *Rubicon*, and for the first time fear intruded on our relationship. My worry meter was finally in the red zone. I felt it just as I reached over the companionway sill to attach the tether of my harness to a pad eye (one of the strongpoints in the cockpit designed for just this purpose). Standing on the steps of the companionway, that transitory space between the safety of the cabin and whatever threats may be waiting on deck, I knew that I wouldn't step into the cockpit without the security of my leash. I also knew that this was one time I didn't want to go there at all. The steady roar of the wind as it chased past the rigging was the soundtrack for a sleigh ride over great black waves. I took a few moments to concentrate on my breathing, adopting that slow and steady cadence that tames the mind and allows you to do what the moment requires.

About halfway through the necessary on-deck inspections, a gap appeared in the cloud cover and the streaming moonlight cast the black hills in sharp relief. As we rode to the tops of these waves, the moon lit the sea around us with deep ravines of menace, and sliding to the troughs I could see the seas rise half the height of Rubicon's 65-foot mast. (Perhaps it was less; there was a lot of salt spray in my eyes.) I hadn't wanted to go on deck, but once there I didn't want to leave. Relishing this ride through the height of an ocean gale on a magnificent thoroughbred, any thought of complaint dissolved into gratitude.

The ocean is partying along this morning, its energy undiminished but slightly less threatening in the light of day. The seas are now colored with a greenish tint and the waves wear feathery hats of white spume. Stretching to the horizon, they seem endless. I'm at the center of nature's finest museum, witness to a seascape that locks you in its grip, commanding the attention of all your senses. The spell is broken as *Rubicon* slides into the trough of a wave and we're surrounded by walls of water, but the curtain soon rises again as we approach the next wave top and I shake my head in wonder. *Rubicon* seems right at home as she drives along.

On the eastbound passage I had done more than my share of deck work, and it was at my own request. I was, after all, trying to get ready for the solo return. One evening when heavy weather was descending I went forward to set the storm jib. It was more of an aerobic exercise than I'd expected, and when I returned to the cockpit I fell onto the bench rather dramatically and exclaimed, "Well, that was no walk in the park." Mike looked at me from under the hood of his rain jacket and without missing a beat said, "Hey, you picked the park, buddy." We both had a good laugh. So why pick this park? Why pick the OSTAR?

The idea of doing an OSTAR had been in my head for years. It was there with thoughts of many things that I will never do, but sometimes it would try to make a break for it, to find a home in that part of the mind where plans are made. Late one evening it succeeded, with some assistance from a tall glass of Dewar's and water. The date is documented because the idea, which was almost a decision, immediately prompted me to e-mail Bill. I asked "hypothetically" about his thoughts on a sail out of Newport *if* I intended to have *Rubicon* in Plymouth, England, no later than May 20, 2009, and in condition to return to Newport around, say, noon on May 25, 2009? There was no turning back after that.

Everyone in the OSTAR needs to articulate a reason for doing the race, if not for themselves, then for their friends and family and anyone else who will ask. I think of George Mallory's three-word answer to why he wanted to climb Mount Everest. "Because it's there," he said, and there is something to that. It is indeed there. I'm also reminded of the quip that economists make forecasts because they are asked, not because they know. But some economists do know, or close enough, and so do some sailors. I think we all want to understand the why in how we direct our time and energy—our lives, really. Articulating it can be hard, and convincing others of its logic may sometimes be harder, but believing the story gives us purpose.

Once again I heard the suggestion that I might be trying to prove something. Well, truth be told, I wouldn't mind proving that I'm the best sailor in this famous and challenging race linking the country of my birth to the country where I have made a life, but that isn't going to happen and I won't be crushed. For me, it is a way to go to a special place in solitude, yet with friends. It is hard to be an amateur astronaut, but you can be an amateur sailor. You can be doing something else with your life, no doubt something greater than sailing, and somehow find the time to do this race.

I want to be competitive in this race, but I need to be realistic. You can't win if you don't really push in this contest, but if you push too hard at the wrong time you won't finish. Knowing how hard you're willing to push yourself is a matter of spirit, or guts, but knowing how hard you can push your boat is a matter of experience. Reaching beyond your comfort level may be courageous, but driving beyond your competence invites disaster.

The legend is that the OSTAR race began with a half-crown wager between two colorful characters, Francis Chichester, later Sir Francis, and Herbert George Hasler, known as Blondie. There is no documentation of the wager, but there is clear evidence that Blondie was the man who came up with the idea. Blondie and Chichester and the third founding father (as Lloyd Foster referred to them in his excellent book *OSTAR*), a man with the exceedingly English name of Jack Odling-Smee, launched the project. They managed to convince the Royal Western Yacht Club, of which Odling-Smee was vice-commodore, and none other than Sir Winston Churchill the commodore, to host the eastern side of the race, which they still do these fifty years later. The New York Yacht Club agreed to host the western side of the race. The American host is now the Newport Yacht Club.

Chichester and Hasler were tough fellows. Chichester served in the Royal Air Force during the war, but had already set a number of flight records, including a solo flight from Australia to Japan in 1931. That one ended in a bad crash that he managed to survive. Perhaps the bravest item in Chichester's biography was his decision to buy a house in London during the height of the bombing. Talk about buying your straw hats in January! It is one thing to risk your life, but risking your economic well-being can be terrifying.

Blondie, more formally Lt. Colonel Herbert George Hasler, DSO, OBE, retired Royal Marines, was cited by Foster as opposed to any requirement that competing boats carry radios. Blondie felt that they might radio for help if they got into trouble and generally create a lot of fuss for everyone. Foster quotes him as saying, "It would be more seemly for the entrant to drown like a gentleman." I'm glad Blondie lost that argument.

The first races were sponsored by the *Observer* newspaper, and so the acronym originally referred to the Observer Singlehanded Trans-Atlantic Race. As it was also the original singlehanded transatlantic race, the name OSTAR was kept after the connection to the newspaper dissolved. The race has evolved over the years. One track has gone professional, with career sailors and megabucks budgets, and is an exciting event, as are many professional sports. The other track, the original OSTAR with its Corinthian spirit of amateur enthusiasts, persists, for which I'm thankful, even if the boats, and perhaps the competitors, are nothing like the originals.

At the end of the day, the draw of racing is easy to understand, whether it's sailboats or anything else. It's nature, not nurture. We humans have always wagered our fortunes and our lives over who was best at one game or another. It must be in the genes. No sailboat can sail directly into the wind. In fact, you generally can't sail much closer than 45 degrees to either side of the wind, which means there is always a 90-degree wedge of the compass that's off-limits. Some boats, particularly race boats, can sail at slightly tighter angles, but they still have a large restricted zone. These hard facts create numerous opportunities for calculation: trade-offs between speed and distance made good in the right direction, questions of time on course before tacking, what influences an approaching weather system might exert, and on and on. Keeping your head in the game is a part of the challenge, and critical for performance.

Sailing as recreation is something else. The recreational yacht has a very limited story in the catalogue of nautical history. No doubt economics explains most of that. You really need a middle class with a bit of disposable income to develop a market for recreational boats, but that begs the question of why do it at all.

There is no doubt that a lot of fun can be had on a sailboat, whether it's taking a day sail on the bay, a weekend trip to a favorite port, or sipping a cocktail as you savor your arrival at a warm Caribbean anchorage. There are, however, many and deeper draws from boats and the sea, and one of the little secrets of passagemaking is that fun often drops to the bottom of the list. You can almost count on some truly sublime moments making their visitations during a passage, but the day to day of dealing with too much wind, or not enough wind, or wind from the wrong direction, or boat problems, or this or that calamity du jour suggests that "fun" is not always the best descriptor.

For some, and for me, one attraction has been to learn the science, and a bit of the art, of sailing, to master the ability to move a big inanimate object from anywhere to somewhere with only the power of the wind, and in a manner that has been used for thousands of years. The depth of the satisfaction has surprised me. Perhaps it's not rocket science—the wind can either push you, which it does when you're sailing downwind with the breeze behind you, or effectively pull you, which it does when you're sailing upwind. The sails act like wings, and as wings they have high-pressure and low-pressure sides as the wind passes over them. By controlling the position and the shape of the sails, the pressure can be directed toward driving the boat. Many books have been written on how sails work, some with a dense crop of equations, but that's basically it; you're getting pulled or you're being pushed, or some combination of the two, just like on land. Competent sailors have the ability to undertake the passages they need to make, and find their way to the next port with a minimum of loss.

No doubt there is an intellectual side to the attraction, but I believe the real lure of blue-water sailing is to experience the great oceans and waterways of our planet in an intimate way, to witness nature in all its moods, to see the heavens without light pollution blotting out the visions, to learn patience and many other things.

The captain of a sailing vessel must be a craftsman who can fashion his boat and his behavior to the rhythms of the sea. At the end of a passage, that ephemeral construction that was the passage goes to memory, where it cures and reflects who you are.

After a dinner of beef stew I settle down with *Stanley and the Women* by Kingsley Amis. I admire Stanley, not because I've experienced any of that sad character's particular misfortunes, but rather for the way he muddles through the chaos and calamity of his life, and for the fact that he's always ready to have a drink with friend or foe.

I'm munching on nuts again. The beef jerky ran out while I was reading my cowboy book.

NIGHT SAILING

*Musicians don't retire; they stop when
there's no more music in them.*

—LOUIS ARMSTRONG

How many places do we travel where any comment on the weather is met with, "If you don't like the weather just wait 5 minutes; it'll change?" I've heard it said in Maine and Florida and points in between. Here, at least you can see the change coming, and it's unfolding before my eyes as the cloud banks roll away and the seas settle down. It was a long wait, measured in days, not hours.

It's a full morning's work on deck with *Rubicon* continually changing her wardrobe as we shake off one reef after another. We now have all our canvas flying. Almost no one uses canvas anymore, but sailors still call it that. Most sails these days are made from some form of manufactured fiber. The sails on *Rubicon* are made of Vectran, a very strong and durable material, if a little heavier than the laminated fabrics used for racing sails.

Wind and waves have moderated. I have taken down and bagged the storm jib and lugged it below to the aft locker. It's now stowed, and hopefully for a while. The big genoa is full and pulling. Other than a brief appearance a couple of days ago, the sun has been hiding for almost a week and its visit today is warm and motivating, a tonic to the spirits. I give the boat a thorough cleanup, starting with the galley, and then place a large pot of chili on the stove to simmer. We've passed the halfway point so it's time to slice into that fruitcake. I brew a large mug of tea to go with a double slice. It's a sweet repast, perhaps made the better for the wait.

Sir Francis Drake once said, "It isn't that life ashore is distasteful to me, but life at sea is better." It's a wonderful line, and given Drake's opportunities for that trifecta of fame, wealth, and glory, he may have been perfectly serious, but I also suspect he may have just been having relationship issues at the time. Life can be hard out here, but you have the luxury to think of all your other problems as secured in their various boxes, the lids screwed tight till you step ashore, until you are back in the world. Or at least that is a fiction you can believe in for a bit. The problems might not be secured at all, but whatever fires may be burning in your land life, they are left to your friends and colleagues, or most likely your better half, to bring under control.

What a day! I have barely touched a line since lunch while *Rubicon* has gracefully put the miles behind her. I'm working on deck in shorts and a T-shirt, and it's a great pleasure to feel the sun on my skin. I should be two-thirds of the way to Newport by now, not halfway, but perhaps we can make up some time in the days ahead. I fill a bowl with chili—simple fare, but the joy of good food on this peaceful evening somehow reminds me of the wonderful last meal I experienced before leaving the corporate world and starting on a new path.

It was perhaps the most welcome meal of my life, and I was enjoying it in the rustic splendor of the Saddle Brook Inn, a few miles from our offices in northern New Jersey. Sunlight flooded the room and glasses tinkled as another toast was offered. It would be the last of the many meals we had enjoyed together.

There were five of us. Christina, the founder and CEO of the firm, was fully on, as always, and justly proud of her accomplishment in building the firm and negotiating a strong sale. There were, oddly enough, three Johns, one the president of the company, the others older gentlemen, retired from their previous lines of work and serving as independent directors on our mutual funds. We had just completed the final board meeting of the funds, as they were being folded into the mutual funds of the bank that had purchased our firm six months previously.

I was the chief operating officer of the firm, but that would end with the luncheon. I had given Chris my resignation letter three months earlier and she had asked me to stay through today's final board meeting.

It was a restrained celebration. The independent directors had lost their part-time jobs, an inevitable result of the fund consolidation and not of great import to them, but they had not been otherwise involved with the firm, so they made no money from the sale. However, they were good men who had exercised their fiduciary obligations with diligence, and they seemed genuinely pleased by the success of the firm.

When I climbed into my car after the lunch, after all the good-byes and the promises to keep in touch, I was in a bit of a daze, and with apologies to the great Dr. Martin Luther King, I mouthed the words, "Free at last, free at last, thank God Almighty, I'm free at last." I was out of work for the first time since I was a boy. With a modicum of prudence, I could remain free of financial worries, and I was free of corporate responsibilities. It was the first day of my new life. It felt delicious, and intoxicating.

Retirement was not a topic I had ever mentioned to my children for the simple reason that it was not something I had particularly desired, expected, or seriously contemplated, but times change. Chief operating officer had a good ring to it, and the job kept me so busy that the months flew by like the flipping calendar pages seen in old movies where the characters are on an express train to a new time in their lives, but I had no love for the COO job. An inside definition of money management is that it's the business of getting and keeping money to manage. Properly structured portfolios may be the product of an investment firm, but there's a lot more to the game. Most of the issues that found their way to my desk were management ones: they covered a wide spectrum of compliance, finance, contract, and human resource questions, but no longer the mysteries of the investment equation. We ran a clean shop, and had no more problems in these areas than the next firm—I'd like to think fewer—but still, there were just so many of them. And they kept coming because we kept growing, and thank God for that. There was money to be made from growth, and money's lovely handmaidens: security and options.

Investment firms generally have a chief investment officer (CIO) to deal with investment strategy, so when I was kicked upstairs those challenges, the intellectual puzzles that link you to the rest of the world and allow your firm to first survive and then prosper, were no longer a part of my brief. From a lifetime of habit and fascination I continued to follow the financial markets, but I was no longer a "market participant" as the financial press labels money managers and their ilk. Somehow I felt less connected because of that. More to the point—much more to the point, actually—after twelve years of helping to build the firm, and three decades in the business, I was burned out. I needed a change, at least for a while.

Amy's reaction to the news was one of delight, in no small part because she had yet to earn her driver's license and quickly realized how chauffeuring would fit into my new job description. Steven, who was driving by then, had a different reaction, and what it may have lacked in tact was made up for in honesty. He just looked at me in surprise and said, "So, ah, Dad, you mean like you're going to be around all the time?" Steve quickly got used to the idea, and it didn't seem to change our relationship greatly. I'm not sure how much difference my being home made in those last couple of years. Perhaps I was just reassuring myself, but those were the postnanny and preadult years where a little extra vigilance is never a bad thing.

Though I had never yearned for early retirement, or expected to see it, I found it the easiest of life's transitions. Despite the fact that the only employment gap I'd had since high school was a long road trip taken during a college summer, the decision seemed so right that I never drafted the list of pros and cons that I usually find necessary before crossing any rubicon. The decision was made during a week of touring the Irish countryside with Barbara and the kids shortly after the firm was sold. Had I contemplated retirement longer, I might have feared it. Ernest Hemingway called retirement "the ugliest word in the English language." The language has grown since he penned those words, but if you're not careful it can still be true. I think my transition was easy because, so far, I have never considered it permanent, and of course I never use the *R* word.

I cannot say I didn't miss the action. I damn well did. I missed the stream of smart people coming into my office to discuss the issues du jour. I missed seeing a team working together to keep the organism that is a growing business focused, healthy, and profitable. I missed having a phenomenal assistant who kept some of the noise away and helped me to look good in the job. And of course I missed dealing with the clients. Institutional investment clients usually understand the financial markets as well as the money managers, sometimes better. Their focus often seemed more outward looking than that of the money managers, less parochial, but I could be wrong about that. And, as anyone who has ever worked in a corporate setting will know, there were things that no sane person would ever miss.

As one of the firm's principals, I was subject to the five-year noncompete clause that was a part of the buyout agreement. Leaving meant that I would be limited in taking another job in the investment world, but that restriction was a gift. I had the great opportunity to step back and consider the next chapter. And that chapter, in addition to a more home-centered parenting of my high school children, involved sailing.

For a while I was downright defensive when the subject of retirement came up. This was not the most socially graceful tack to take with friends, particularly those who were still working, and I regret it now. They didn't always see the seriousness of what I was doing, but I was learning the art of sailing, not just the basic mechanics. After the OSTAR I will need to find the next chapter. Sailing will always be a part of my life, but it is not enough. It's no doubt high time to find a vehicle for some giveback for the good luck I've had, or at least a way to make a buck, or both would be nice. Without that next chapter, I will wake up one morning and find myself retired.

Retirement in the twenty-first century is not your father's retirement. With a modicum of health, financial resources, and imagination, a great retirement can be built, but the building must be a unique creation. You must decide how best to employ your talents and rehire yourself; in a sense one must be rehired, not retired. And the why of it is because, apart from children or spouses, no one really expects much of you if you're labeled a retiree. The rest of society is quite content if you simply pay your bills and respect the traffic laws. You have to write your own job description and then expect something from yourself.

I have just stepped on deck for a quick look around before making a midnight entry in the log and I'm captured by the night. A night whose quiet is the perfect counterpoint to yesterday's shrieking wind. I look up at the mast, set against uncountable stars, bathed in the Milky Way, and a deep sense of peace washes over me. The heavenly display transfixes and thoughts turn as crisp as the night sky. I cannot imagine being in a place with a greater power to move the soul. I don't know how long I stand in the cockpit, one hand holding the rail over the dodger, locked in the embrace of this sublime moment. Then I lower my gaze and see the boat, a magnificent machine, the workings of which have been perfected over a thousand years and more. I feel privileged to be on it. I feel as if I am seeing it for the first time. I'm thinking it's one of those can't-be-improved moments when the thought occurs to step below and queue up Louis Armstrong singing "What a Wonderful World." Who can listen to his joyful interpretation of that song and not smile?

Eventually the brain intrudes, an unwanted guest. The clarity begins to fade. I know that what I am looking at has no more clarity than the rest of my life. Some of the stars I think I see have been dead for millions of years, their last light still streaming in from journeys started multimillions of light years ago. Those shows are over; the stage lights just haven't come down yet. On other stages, new stars have been born but it may be a while before those lights go up on this planet.

My peak moment has passed—why are they always so brief?—but I'm still affected by the peace of here as I polish off another bowl of chili. A beer would be nice, but it really doesn't get much better.

WATCHING
THE RADIO

*That fat speed that I love, that
sensation, that's what I want.*

—PICABO STREET

The wind has gone light again, and we're on the verge of being becalmed but still moseying along in the right direction. Why doesn't this get boring? The great sailor and writer Bernard Moitessier once wrote, "I hate storms, but calms undermine my spirits." Ain't that the truth. But of course, as Moitessier knew, between those two ends of the spectrum lies the vast joy of sailing. When you're not scared or going crazy, life on a sailboat can be sublime.

Stocks of corned beef hash (canned of course), eggs, and coffee still fill one of the lockers and cooking is easy as we sidle along. The sea has lost her whitecaps, and she's dressed this morning in one of her dark blue suits. The sun is drying and warming the cockpit. It is a grand day for dining, and I stretch out the meal as long as conscionable while considering the day's priorities beyond staying on track for the finish.

I am fortunate that my little fire in the wiring a few days ago did not affect the GPS feed to the VHF radio, and so the unit still displays my current position. A nice feature, and very handy when I'm making notations in the log, plotting my position on the chart, or just want to know where I am. The radio shows our position to three decimal places, and it doesn't take long for the number located three places out from the decimal to change. That's the one showing changes of one thousandth of a nautical mile, and it's the hook. I've found myself staring at the changing thousandths of a minute in the longitude and latitude boxes for long periods, munching on pretzels or an apple and watching the digits tick by.

A minute of longitude is an arc equal to one sixtieth of a degree, a tiny segment of the 360 degrees of arc circling our planet. A minute of longitude, east or west, varies as the meridians of longitude converge at the poles, but one minute of the arc of latitude, north or south along any meridian of longitude, is the definition of a nautical mile, and it's a constant, or it would be if the earth were a perfect sphere. It is close enough to a constant that the agreement to peg it to exactly 1,852 meters, reached in 1929 at the International Hydrographic Conference, still holds. In any event, if both these numbers are increasing at roughly the same rate I know we are headed northwest, and if the latitude number is increasing and the longitude number dropping, then I know that we have somehow gotten ourselves turned around and are headed back to Plymouth. If one number is changing faster than another, the direction can be fine-tuned, from, say, northwest to west-northwest.

With this new awareness in mind, I can spend a minute staring at the numbers, their direction of change and their rate of change, and get a sense of our heading. It's an approximation, but if it's three in the morning and raining, and we're well trimmed and moving, that approximation may be good enough. The alternative is to go on deck and check the compass at the helm. Thank God for the magnetic compass—the most reliable of tools with no modern technology in it, except perhaps for the hardened glass covering the swinging compass card. I've heard that some buyers of new boats are omitting the magnetic compass, reasoning that their electronic chartplotters and instruments will deliver the same information and more. This is a sensible approach as long as you don't plan to leave the dock. The magnetic compass has been around since the twelfth century. It's a great run for a piece of technology and it has yet to be rendered obsolete, or optional.

Speed could also be determined by the radio's readout. One could look at the unit for a minute, calculate the distance covered, and multiply by sixty to determine the boat's speed in knots, or nautical miles, per hour. However, calculating the distance covered gets a little tricky unless you're simply sailing along one of the meridians of longitude, or parallels of latitude, so the hard number remains elusive. What I do glean is a rough idea of our speed, which I add to the other evidence—the way the sails are drawing, the movement of the boat through the water, and our angle of heel. From this I get an acceptably accurate number for entry in the ship's log, and throughout the day for peace of mind when I ask myself if we are moving quickly enough.

I would certainly prefer the precision of a hard number because I didn't leave all my neurosis on land, though I would not be going any faster with this knowledge. There are two handheld GPS units onboard that can quickly calculate our speed over the ground, or SOG, which in the absence of any influence from the currents is also the boat speed or speed through the water. I power one up periodically to confirm my senses, but I can't use the unit 24/7 or I would soon have a bin of dead batteries and no backup GPS.

The sensation of speed can be an intoxicant, but the absolute speed never defines the experience. The average speed on the Kansas Turnpike is faster than most roller coaster rides, but the sensation of speed on the roller coaster trumps the car ride past the cornfields. Speeds at sea never sound fast by land standards (except for some wind speeds!). All else equal, the longer the boat, the higher its maximum speed. This number is defined as its hull speed, and is a function of the length of the hull at the waterline. Running downwind in big waves can cause a sailboat to exceed her hull speed for a time as she surfs down the waves. Great fun, but watch your steering! I've had *Rubicon* over 10 knots only a handful of times, and usually average considerably less, but out here you feel the movement of every mile under the hull. I will no doubt invest more hours of my life crammed into the belly of a jumbo jet, but I doubt I will ever feel as near to flying as when I'm on the deck of a sailboat. And when she has a bone in her teeth—as sailors like to say—and she's carving a path through the sea at her hull speed, the thrill is visceral. It's satisfying to get your boat moving in light winds, but the sailing high comes in fresher winds, when your boat is driving through the sea on the best line to the mark, locked in the groove. You can feel the pulse of the boat and it can bring a primal yell of joy to the lungs.

My nav station may not be the rich information center it was at the beginning of the race, but I still have my computer, which keeps me in touch with the world, AIS to alert me to any ships in the neighborhood, and the radio, which is quiet in midocean but captivates me with its seductive display. If someone had told me that halfway through the race I'd be looking at the radio to learn my course and speed, I would have laughed. Now I'm grateful that we are on course, and I will gladly use whatever tools I can find to keep it that way.

Today's e-mail brings a note from Barbara reporting that all's well on the home front. She also reports that Jan Kees Lampe, a Dutchman sailing a race boat called *La Promesse*, has already crossed the finish line. His boat certainly lived up to its name. He gets line honors for being the first in, but the winner, and the rankings in this year's OSTAR, will be based on corrected times, and those are determined based on the rating of each boat. There is a complicated handicapping system in sailboat racing that attempts to put all the boats on a level playing field by assigning per-mile time adjustments to each boat. The adjustments are usually so many seconds per mile, and they are determined by formulas based on each boat's specifications. *Rubicon* doesn't get much help from this system and shouldn't need much. Though not a race boat, she is a fast cruiser, the slow progress of this passage notwithstanding.

I admit to mixed feelings that the lead boats are already arriving. Of course, they are purebred race boats, and most of the fleet could never keep up with them. Still, I had hoped to be closer. I'm beginning to suspect that one of my strategic mistakes in this race was to fully adopt the "run your own race" strategy. It worked in the Bermuda Race, but that was a much shorter race, and it was one time, and of course an element of luck was involved. It's dawning on me that without knowing where the other boats are, particularly those in my class, I've allowed the various problems on the boat to put me more in a delivery mode, rather than race mode. I could have asked someone to send me a daily report of all boat positions, which one can get from the website, and perhaps that would have added the extra burn to pick off a boat in front, or avoid being passed from behind.

After sitting becalmed for a couple of hours at midday, we've been doing the slow glide all afternoon in wispy winds. It's still necessary to run the engine in neutral every day to keep the batteries charged, but it usually doesn't take much more than an hour. The only real power drains now are the radio, sitting silently in standby mode, and the navigation lights at night. This is certainly not the ideal time to be reducing my carbon footprint, but I seem to have broken all of the onboard energy hogs. As with many Americans, I would like to go green, just not right now.

Dr. Samuel Johnson once said, "When men come to like a sea life, they are not fit to live on land." I hope that was one of the things the great doctor was wrong about, because today was grand, a day filled with the peace of slow sailing, and I have come to like a sea life. How many days on land would I have been content with slow progress in the right direction, especially if the stage were set with the beauty of today?

I am done for today with pondering the mysteries of the sea and turn to *Stanley and the Women*. It chronicles the chapter in Stanley's life where his grown son is hospitalized with blooming schizophrenia, but the story is really about Stanley's relationships with the women in his life: current wife, ex-wife, friend, and son's doctor. These interactions reveal what might be called the Neanderthal tendencies of Stanley, and of a couple of the women for that matter. I find it a sad book, as Stanley keeps swinging away, trying for connection.

THE HAT TRICK

People change and forget to tell each other.
—LILLIAN HELLMAN

There was another sailboat on the horizon at first light, perhaps another competitor in the OSTAR, but he didn't respond to my radio call. He probably thought he was alone out here and had the radio turned off. We are not moving at any great turn of speed, but it is a nice downwind sail. It is surprising how much downwind sailing there has been in what is essentially an upwind passage against the prevailing westerlies. I consider flying the spinnaker. Spinnakers are those large, light, and colorful sails so adept at catching the breeze on a downwind run. There have been other times I should have flown the spinnaker, but they can be tricky sails to keep properly set and my energies have been rather fully consumed with the other demands of this OSTAR.

The weather is spectacular but so bright that I can't work on deck without sunglasses. Shorts and a T-shirt complete the uniform of the day. I have finished reading *Stanley and the Women* and I am stuck in a loop of thoughts about Barbara, the second woman in my life that I have come to view as my better half.

I had agreed to go on another blind date. It was the second friend who had approached me and said, "I realize it's not quite a year yet, but I know this woman who would be great for you." I had accepted the first time, mainly because I was lonely and craved some adult conversation that was not in the office and about business. That evening had been pleasant but there were no fireworks.

This time when the door opened I was greeted by an attractive petite woman with blond hair, blue eyes, a ready smile, and the legs of a dancer. Barbara lived about an hour's drive away, so I had suggested she pick the restaurant.

We both decided on the fillet of sole. I remember saying, "Perhaps this means we'll be soul mates," and immediately thinking that it was too forward a thing to say, not to mention being very corny, but not regretting it. The truth is we did become soul mates, though not that night. After a bit of probing I learned that she was a principal at a special-education high school, that she was also a single parent (though her daughter was already away at college), that she had put herself through college and graduate school while working full time and raising her daughter alone, and, perhaps most important, that she had a sense of humor. Whatever rules of dating I once knew were pretty rusty, but impulsively I gave her a quick kiss on the lips as we said goodnight and told her I wanted to see her again.

It has been a long romance and one that has grown slowly. We dated for seven years before I proposed marriage, and when I did propose I wanted the moment to be grand. It was grand indeed, a night for the memory banks.

We were booked on the dinner cruise down the Seine and we barely made it as the Parisian subway experienced an unexplained stop of such duration that we had to run the last half-mile to the dock. We both arrived in our best travel outfits, but dripping with sweat and Barbara none too pleased that I had sounded like a drill instructor as I hurried us to the boat.

"Come on, Barbara, we gotta step it up or we'll miss the boat."

"For God's sake, I think we can find a decent restaurant in Paris if we miss the damn boat!" she said. "Maybe *you* should try running in high heels!"

Fortunately, as the wide and comfortable dinner barge motored quietly through the city, the white tablecloths, violinists, and spectacular views of Paris gave space for our moods to change; our sweat dried as we sipped glasses of white wine.

It was our second-to-last night in Paris, and my last good opportunity to pull off a memorable wedding proposal. After all, how ridiculous would it be to spend a week in Paris and then wind up proposing back in New Jersey? Not to mention the discomfort of walking around Paris all week with a diamond ring in my pocket, particularly as Paris shares the fate of many European cities in hosting a large population of pickpockets. I've sometimes wondered why we don't have such a problem in the United States, and I think it's because we like to stay in our cars. In any event, I was determined that they were not going to find my cache.

I'm not sure why it was so important to me that it be done just right, perhaps because it would be my second marriage, and hopefully my last, but whatever the reason, form had taken an outsized role and all it took was four tries over the course of the week.

During my first attempt, and certainly the most picturesque, we were in the opulent gardens of Versailles. I had just put my mind in the proper focus for a marriage proposal when Barbara, her hair rapidly expanding in the humid air, exclaimed, "It's so hot all I can think about is finding some air conditioning!" It *was* hot. The heat wave that month had taken the lives of many Parisians, and it certainly took the life from that moment.

On my second try, we were in a fine restaurant and had just finished a meal that had us thinking of learning French and emigrating. I was primed and had my hand on the ring when I looked up to see a waiter scurrying by. I watched as two bread rolls slid off his tray, took a short flight, and bounced loudly off the china on our table. In the ensuing bustle of apologies and table clearing, the mood shifted, and mood is everything in these things. I decided to wait.

The third attempt was almost a wrap. We were in a small jazz bar with subdued lighting. A bluesy musician was playing a soft saxophone, very Paris. I was thinking this could work, when a very large man and his three-woman entourage entered the scene. After landing at the table next to us, the choreography unfolded as packs of cigarettes and various lighters were retrieved from pockets and purses. Within moments we were in a fog of tobacco smoke. As ex-smokers, we had even less tolerance for the habit than most. We looked at each other and decided to call it a night. The Seine cruise was the last good opportunity.

This time, after the plates from the main course had been cleared and we sat watching the cathedral of Notre Dame slide into view, I knew it was time to green-light the project. I took Barbara's hand and asked her how she liked the small ruby ring she was wearing that night. "You know I like this ring," she said, no doubt thinking it was an odd question as I had given her the ring two years earlier as a Christmas present. I then put the box with the engagement ring on the table, opened it in her direction, and asked, "Do you like this one better?" It was as close as I ever came to a Clark Gable moment. We hadn't thought anyone else had noticed, but were happily surprised by a small round of applause as we rose to leave at the end of the evening.

Barbara accepted my proposal. We were engaged, though it would be three more years before we shared a home, and we never married. The marriage proposal had not broken our stalemate. I suppose I was naïve to think it would. We faced the same impasse that had stalled earlier discussions. Life went on as before, except that we were engaged.

Our stalemate was geographic. I would not move from the town where I lived until my children graduated from high school. Their grandparents lived in the town, and I felt the children had enough to process without moving to another school system in their high school years. Barbara felt that moving to "my town" reflected too much compromise on her part, particularly as she had already raised her daughter. She also objected to the commute, which was a tad longer. Barbara suggested we find a new town between our two homes. That was her compromise. My compromise was an offer to move anywhere after the children graduated, but nowhere until that came to pass. I purchased a beautiful older home in a lovely section of Westfield, both as an inducement and because the English Tudor, built in the thirties and sheathed in warm bricks, looked like it could be our Ponderosa. In the end we both stuck to our guns in our "negotiations," and we ended where we started.

When Amy graduated from high school our stalemate finally ended, though our relationship was battle scarred by that point, and of course we were both different people. Our stalemate had produced stale mates. With both of my children in possession of their diplomas, I was willing to leave Westfield, and I suggested we look in the towns we had discussed earlier, but new variables had entered the scene. Barbara's daughter and son-in-law had purchased a house about a mile from her and now had two young sons. Barbara's new position was that we should live in her area, the northern suburbs of New Jersey. The idea of a fresh location was off the table. Barbara had logic, as well as every grandmother in America, on her side, but it struck me as a failure of equity and I harbored a grudge. No doubt what I really resented was that I had flown solo for so long. Not solo exactly—Barbara had been a big help and I had the nannies for the earlier years—but it felt like a solo flight. What would I have done if the situation had been reversed? I never dwelled on the question.

We had been looking at houses for about a month when, one week into the spring of that year, Barbara called me from her office to say that her doctor had referred her to an oncologist. She was frightened, and so was I. We met with the doctor who informed us of the discovery of a large tumor on one of Barbara's ovaries. The doctor said that it was too dangerous to biopsy the tumor, and that it would need to be removed before we learned if it was lethal or benign. He was kind, but unwilling to share any optimism he might have felt. I shuddered inside, but Barbara had enough optimism, and courage, for all of us. The operation was scheduled before we left his office.

It was a busy season. It was the spring of our house hunting, the spring of Barbara's tumor, and the spring of the on and off and back-on plans to do the Bermuda 1-2 Race, and we did a hat trick. After the big scare and a major operation for Barbara, her tumor was benign, we found a house in her preferred location, and I competed in the race.

I now believe that in the two biggest "compromise or don't compromise" decisions of my life, I compromised once and rejected compromise once and I was wrong on both occasions.

As a man still young, but closing in on thirty, I compromised and bought my first home in New Jersey with my bride, who didn't care for city living, thus assuring that my dream of finishing my PhD would evaporate. It was time to begin making mortgage payments, not a time to quit my job and write a dissertation. I would not be an economist. All of us carry a basket of losses with us, and that is one of mine. Even in my most grandiose moments I cannot believe that the world is any the worse for this outcome. Nevertheless, it was a disappointment.

With Barbara, I refused to compromise and move during the children's high school years. Now, reflecting on Barbara's ability to connect with children, her understanding of the many and varied questions of parenting, and the love she felt for Amy and Steven, I've come to believe that the children would have been better served had we all lived together, whatever the short-term disruption. Their high school years escaped the turbulence of relocation, but the new life that I passed on could have been a treasure chest of love and opportunity. That's what economists call "opportunity cost," the cost of not reaping what might have been.

In the movie *It's a Wonderful Life*, George Bailey (Jimmy Stewart) saw many of his dreams go unfulfilled, but there came a time when he was able—albeit through the intervention of an angel—to look back and accept how lucky he'd been, and see what a wonderful life he'd led. One day, when my children are flying—happy in their work, secure in their financial footings, and on a path to knowledge and comfort with who they really are—I have little doubt that I'll be echoing Jimmy Stewart. I have had a wonderful life. When I've banished the last of my demons of regret, those benighted occupation troops that darken your spirits and poison your future, I will no doubt embrace the truth of my good fortune.

I still believe in the seminal importance of compromise. Relationships can't exist without it. Civilization declines without it. There are moments when a failure to compromise closes the road to progress. There are, of course, moments to stand fast, and those must also be honored. I just wish I could tell the little fuckers apart!

We are flying, powering along under the full main and genoa. No reefs tonight and no clouds on the horizon. I eat lightly and skip the music. My mind is cluttered as *Rubicon* carves a path toward home.

YA GOTTA LOVE IT

Beware the fury of a patient man.

—JOHN DRYDEN

'm a patient man. I think I learned it during a long business career, or maybe it was in my marriage or parenting; yes, that was it, parenting. In any event, it takes a lot to make me really lose it. This morning did it.

The day started out well enough with *Rubicon* moving along briskly in a clear morning, all sails flying. After a bit I noticed that Hydro was having trouble keeping a proper course, and the culprit was an unbalanced rig. I had rolled up some of the big genoa during the night when the wind came up, so I had a small headsail while I was still flying the full mainsail. It seemed like a good idea to put a reef in the main, roll up the genoa completely, and fly the solent sail with one reef. Hydro and I have been enjoying a fine relationship, and Hydro steers a pretty good course most of the time, except for some reason when I'm napping, in which case it likes to shift the course 40 to 50 degrees and see if I notice when I wake up. The obvious answer of course would be to avoid napping during wind shifts, as a wind vane sails the boat at a constant angle to the wind, but I haven't been able to synchronize my sleep schedule yet.

Apart from catching me napping, the one area of our relationship that still needs work is reefing. When you're putting in a reef, or shaking one out, you are changing the boat's sail wardrobe and her trim. I've noticed that Hydro doesn't like this in-between phase. An autopilot would simply steer you right through this transitory period. As you can't hand steer, adjust the wind vane, and work on the foredeck all at the same time, it presents a bit of a problem, but so far, with some alacrity on my part and some tolerance on Hydro's part, we've always been able to accomplish the task. Not so this morning. I had eased the mainsheet and gone to the mast when Hydro decided it would be fun to jibe the boat. With the preventer set, the boom wasn't going too far but with the mainsheet eased, the upper part of the mainsail flopped over and I heard a series of reports—reports as in bang, bang, bang—as my three Dutchman lines were taken out in about the time it takes to say bang, bang, bang. (The Dutchman is a neat little arrangement that drops a series of monofilament lines from various points on the topping lift down through the mainsail. It allows the sail to drop like a venetian blind, either partway for reefing or all the way.) I looked up to see wisps of monofilament line trailing from the topping lift like tinsel on a discarded Christmas tree. I let out a long sigh. I'm a patient man.

The loss of the Dutchman lines was not a breakage of any major consequence. It's not a critical system, and a couple of hours at the dock with a spool of monofilament line will restore it to good order. However, having sailed the boat for five years and thousands of miles without blowing out the lines, having it happen now was very annoying. A short argument ensued with Hydro and I'm happy to report that I got the last word in.

The next order of the day was to set the solent sail with a reef in it, so I went to the bow, tied in all the reef pendants holding up the foot of the sail, and went to hoist the sail. I then noticed that one of these short pendant lines had come out when it was last flown, so I quickly took a piece of line from my pocket and tied it in. The job was interrupted when an outsized wave rocked the boat, but then quickly finished. Unfortunately, I had made an incredible rookie mistake when I threw that last line through the grommet to finish tying up the foot of the sail. I had failed to notice that the little rope was wrapped around the lower lifeline. It's always a good idea to check your preparations before the action begins, but it's a step I omitted after that last seemingly trivial task. I saw my error as I began hauling away on the halyard to raise the sail, but it was too late. My moment of recognition was time enough for the wind to catch the sail and deliver an 18-inch tear to the fabric. I'm a patient man, so I just let out a long groan before lowering the sail back down.

The solent isn't the most vital sail in the inventory, but it is an important one and would have been perfect for today. Repairs can no doubt be made without too much difficulty. However, the breeze was picking up and I really wanted to get the show on the road, so I gave that task a short postponement. The only alternative was to call out the reserve force, the trusty storm jib, so I retrieved that sail from the lazarette, hanked it to the stay above the torn solent, and sent it into action.

When all this activity was completed the boat was moving nicely again, though not as smartly as she would have been with the proper sail. As I sat down in the cockpit to take a little break and enjoy the balmy weather, I put on my Rangers cap and looked up to survey the sails. In the next moment the wind grabbed my cap, along with the hat clip that I had not yet secured to my shirt, and delivered it to the sea. That's when I lost it. The expletives flew fast and thick, and were no doubt picked up by a few Coast Guard stations. It's a good thing there was no one else on the boat, but come on, enough is enough!

As I ponder the events of this morning, I realize that in return for about three hours of work on deck I've generated at least four hours of repair work. It is rather disheartening, particularly as I had started to consider my Rangers hat as my lucky cap, but there are lessons in all of this. When the frustration has worn off, I'll consider them.

Right now we're south of the Flemish Cap, the exotically named eastern cusp of the Grand Banks featured so prominently in *The Perfect Storm*. I had hoped to be farther north at this point, on a shorter line to the finish, but winds and currents have prevented that, so we're still in deep water and we'll skirt the southern borders of the Grand Banks until we cross Georges Bank.

■ ■ ■

The Grand Banks are a series of underwater plateaus on the continental shelf. They extend out from the coast of Newfoundland
to the deep waters of the Atlantic, and a few hours of sailing can
take you from waters over 2 miles deep onto the banks, which
average just under 200 feet in depth. On the chart these areas of
elevated seabed are labeled the Grand Banks of Newfoundland, and
they include such banks as St. Pierre's, but there are a number of
other banks extending down the coast. Farther to the southeast are
the banks off Nova Scotia, with such lovely names as Sable Island
Bank, Lahave Bank, and Emerald Bank. And farther still, there is
Georges Bank, named by English colonists for St. George and sitting squarely in our path to Newport.

Two of the world's great currents, the Gulf Stream and the
much cooler Labrador Current, come together over the Grand
Banks. The offspring of these hot- and cold-blooded rivers, as they
mix with the atmosphere and each other, can grow into dramatic
weather systems, but far more frequently they yield a blanket of fog.
Below the surface, the impact of these divergent currents, as they
mix in the shallower confines of the banks, is the rapid growth of
plankton, that staple in the food chain of marine life.

The first European to set foot on Newfoundland was Leif
Ericksson, the Icelander who arrived around the year 1000.
Unfortunately for Leif, he didn't claim the land for his home
country or get a lot of publicity. The result was that the European
most associated with the discovery of Newfoundland—that is,
the one who saw the land, met the natives, and brought the news
back to the Old World—is usually considered to be John Cabot, a
contemporary of Columbus who landed there in 1497.

Cabot is also credited with discovering the Grand Banks,
which should not be surprising as you can't get to Newfoundland
from Europe without crossing them, but does ignore the fact
that Basque fishermen had apparently traveled great distances to
fish these waters for many years before John Cabot showed up.
But again, Cabot reported his discovery while the Basques kept
these phenomenal fishing grounds a closely held secret. Cabot's
descriptions of the massive cod stocks in these waters are fascinating.

Great codfish of 6 to 7 feet and weighing up to 200 pounds were not uncommon, and he reported that you could catch cod by simply dipping a wicker basket in the water. No cod of that size can be found today, thanks to generations of overfishing.

Oil and gas production is of greater economic interest today than cod fishing, but that may not always be the case. Whether the decimated cod population will survive modern fishing techniques is at best an open question, but we know for sure that the oil is not a renewable resource.

It is a good sail in the afternoon; we are cruising along at I'm guessing somewhere approaching 7 knots with the storm jib and the reefed main. Dinner is a can of vegetable soup bulked up with a few slabs of Wasa crispbread. I don't know how they can call this stuff bread—it looks more like cardboard from a packing carton—but after a while it really does grow on you. It seems the right dinner to enjoy as I'm listening to Bob Seger's "Against the Wind." This OSTAR is all about running against the wind, and not just the prevailing westerlies.

My mood has mellowed. Today's problems are minor and quite repairable, and despite the heavy weather, there have not been any serious gear setbacks for a week, though the earlier ones are more than enough to last me. I think of a comment made by my old friend Mark years ago. We were reviewing client portfolios after a particularly tough day in the market when he just looked at me, smiled, and said, "Ya gotta love it."

A RIVER IN THE SEA

*Men go back to the mountains, as they go
back to sailing ships at sea, because in the
mountains and on the sea they must face up.*
—HENRY DAVID THOREAU

It was a fast sail overnight—close-hauled, sailing quickly with a double-reefed main and the storm jib. There was too much wind for the big genoa, and because I have yet to tackle the sail repair job on the torn solent, I was forced to fly the smallest headsail in the inventory. I'm sure it never blew more than 30 knots, so we were too conservatively canvased. Chalk up another demerit for this OSTAR.

It's a Monday, and the beginning of week four of my race, the week I had been anticipating as arrival week, but now, with over a thousand miles to go, this is not looking likely. The boat could do it, but it would require the right conditions and the right sailing, and would, all in all, be a major stepping-up of the pace. When I think back on the week just passed, I realize it has been nothing but eat, sleep, and sail, though the days have been very different. A week ago we were setting up for heavy weather and by last Wednesday we were in a full-on gale, so it was basically hunker down and work the boat as necessary. Thursday followed with one of the most pleasant of sailing days. Not particularly fast, but smooth as the seas calmed down, the reefs came out, and we settled on our course. Friday, we

were becalmed or barely moving for a large part of the day, but that
soon passed and Saturday was another gift of a day with sun, warmth,
and miles under the keel. Sunday, after I took the time to break a few
things on deck, was a fine day of sailing with *Rubicon*, and today I am
happily in the groove. Last night we entered the Gulf Stream.

The Gulf Stream is often easy to identify, and today there is no
disguising it. The sky is overcast, the air is humid, and the sea is
rough, but not too uncomfortable for this "river in the sea," as Ben
Franklin called it. The Gulf Stream is one of the world's major
ocean currents and some sections can be over a hundred miles
wide. The current runs from Florida northward up the eastern
coast of the United States. North of Cape Hatteras, it runs more
northeast than north as it heads toward the Grand Banks. Once past
the Grand Banks, it splits in two with its main branch, referred to
as the North Atlantic Current or Drift, heading toward the British
Isles. This current helps to explain why Britain is fairly temperate
even though it occupies the same latitudes as Newfoundland and
Labrador. The warm current can run up to 3 knots, and if there is
a strong wind blowing against the current, it will not be too many
hours before life on a small sailboat becomes quite unpleasant. Fortunately, there are no menacing waves today, and we should be
safely beyond its grasp by this time tomorrow.

The Gulf Stream was discovered by Ponce de Leon, the Spanish
explorer now mainly remembered for his quest to find the fountain
of youth. It was mapped by Benjamin Franklin, who published a
chart of the Gulf Stream as early as 1770. If Franklin had done
nothing else in his life, he might have been remembered for this
achievement, but he led such a remarkable life of accomplishment
that this critical mapping exercise is a little remembered footnote
of his story.

The age of sail may be long past, but the Gulf Stream retains a
vital significance for mariners. The largest of ships and the smallest
of oceangoing sailboats still try to hitch a ride in the stream if
they are heading up the coast and going with the flow, or avoid its
countercurrents if they are heading more south and west, and the
savings are counted in time, fuel, and comfort. In the days before

the English figured out the extent and force of this current, their ships made many slow passages to the New World. What makes the Gulf Steam so challenging is not just its propensity to shift position, both seasonally and, seemingly, when the whim takes it, but also the presence of multiple eddies within the stream. There are cold eddies, which are large pools of cold water with a counterclockwise circulation, and warm eddies, which have a clockwise rotation. These eddies can be many miles wide and move both with and within the stream. The result is that at any moment you can be surprised by the arrival of a current from any quarter. Satellite mapping, a tool Franklin would have loved, does an excellent job of tracking this data, which is nice to know given the Gulf Stream's critical role in the ecology of our planet.

Knowledgeable sailors will delay their departure, or modify their routes, if conditions in the Gulf Stream are believed to be treacherous—winds out of the north or northeast against the stream's north-flowing current. These conditions can create tall breaking waves, and they will be more closely spaced than typically found in deep water. A breaking wave is one where the top literally breaks off and falls. It can definitely spoil your day if these big fellas start to fall on your boat. One cubic foot of wave holds 7.5 gallons of water, and each gallon weighs more than 8 pounds. Even the broken-off top of a large wave can be heavy enough and forceful enough to damage a ship, so sailors treat them with respect. In certain conditions, the barrier that is the Gulf Stream should not be approached. Prudent seamanship requires patience without procrastination, and suffers deliberate delay without dithering.

The winners of the Newport to Bermuda yacht race are often those who, either by design or from the smile of fortune, find a quick path across the stream. Because anywhere on the East Coast of the United States is south of Plymouth, the Gulf Stream is far more a barrier than a comfort on this passage.

I've tried to teach my children that everyone faces barriers on their way to achieving the life they want to live. The particulars may change, and new obstacles can arrive at any time, but often the personal barriers make their acquaintance early and stay over the years as unwanted guests. My biggest barriers have been mental, which might be a universal statement now that I think about it. More specifically, mine have been with depression and OCD (obsessive-compulsive disorder). I learned strategies in my twenties to keep my depressions at bay, and the OCD has never approached the level of Jack Nicholson's in the movie *As Good as It Gets*, though it has stolen countless hours of my life.

Gail's barrier was epilepsy, or a seizure disorder as everyone preferred to call it. In earlier times, epileptics were thought of as people possessed by demons, and some shadow of unacceptability has plagued the name. Gail never said she couldn't do this or that because of the barrier that was her epilepsy, or any other. It did take her life, but she damn well lived her life until that moment. I think I know what my children's barriers are. Doesn't every parent? They won't power past them every day, but my parent's prayer is for them to find their strategies to navigate over, around, or through whatever barriers they may face. Perhaps they will reach a point where they will agree with Goldie Hawn, who said, "We have to embrace obstacles to reach the next stage of joy."

Today's download of e-mails and weather charts brings some good news. The weather picture suggests a little rough-and-tumble in the week ahead, coupled perhaps with some opportunities for decent progress, but the e-mails from friends are the most welcome. They go a long way toward canceling my disappointment that this year's plan A—a class win, coupled with honor and glory—has turned to dust. Checking for e-mails is not a long or cumbersome production, but I generally limit myself to twice a day. I'm trying to stay concentrated on the race.

Receiving the daily batch of e-mails reminds me of mail call in the Marines. In those days we had no e-mail and no mobile phones. In fact, for an enlisted marine overseas there was no available phone, period. The only communication was snail mail, but it was reliable. Well, there was the MARS (military affiliate radio station) unit, where every month or so you could make a call. It was quite an operation. The calls went out over high-frequency radios, and were forwarded by local ham (amateur) radio operators around the United States until they were linked into the local phone system.

As your conversation went out over a radio, the radio operator in the next room would periodically flip a switch between transmit and receive. He knew when to do this because he was listening to the conversation, and would switch each party from transmit to receive when they said "over." So the conversation would always begin, "Hi, Mom, how are you? Over." It was a short and stilted conversation, but far superior to no conversation. It was lovely to hear Mom's voice on the other end of the line.

I have discovered a large bag of cookies while rummaging at the back of the food lockers. With most of the fresh food gone, a few treats are nice and I leave the cockpit scattered with crumbs as we power through the night.

PLANET WATER

Do your duty in all things,
you cannot do more, you
should never wish to do less.

—ROBERT E. LEE

feel a bit like Gene Kelly this morning, though less nattily attired, as I dance around in the rain going nowhere. I may not be dancing exactly, but after all this time on the boat, plus the definite loss of a few pounds, I've become quite agile as I move about, hopping from job to job.

I'm guessing it was our approach to a frontal boundary, but the wind died during the night. Actually it wasn't quite dead, just too skittish to harness. I went on deck around two this morning to see the Windex at the top of the mast doing lazy 360-degree revolutions as *Rubicon* rocked in the swells. The Windex is a small weathervane that points toward where the wind is coming from. You can't do much sailing without a definable wind direction, but by dawn the wind had found its direction. By then it was also raining, one of those steady soakers, but the wind was back, so it was don the foulies and trim the boat for whatever speed was possible.

I've been trying hard to get this show on the road for a while—since Plymouth, now that I think about it. However, new reasons have emerged to make haste. I've consumed my last piece of fruitcake, I've managed to avoid the fuss that would have accompanied a very quick finish, and, last but not least, Barbara has sent me an e-mail saying that the boys and girls are starting to bring their boats in now and playtime is over. Of course she didn't phrase it quite like that, but they are and it is. As Captain Renault might have said, "They're all excellent reasons, but you still need an exit visa."

Rubicon is getting a freshwater rinse as the sky releases its torrents. If it were still cold, this would be pretty miserable, but covered in Gore-Tex and seaboots it is not unpleasant as I watch the rivulets of rain flowing from me. It's been coming down hard all day, and life on deck is wet, wet, wet, but it's still dry and cozy in the cabin despite a couple of small leaks that have developed near one of the hatches; nothing of any real concern or inconvenience, but another item for the never-ending repair list.

So much water and none of it is new. The planet doesn't make new water; it's all recycled through the hydrologic cycle. We have approximately 1.4 billion cubic kilometers of water in our planetary inheritance, which from where I'm sitting looks about right. In any event, it is a lot of water. Rather inconveniently, only about 3 percent of the whole splash is fresh water. This may have been an intelligent design, but I'm not seeing it right now.

Schoolchildren have grown up learning that there are four oceans on the planet: the Atlantic, Pacific, Indian, and Arctic. Some learned there were five, having been taught that the Atlantic, the second largest, could be viewed as two oceans, the North Atlantic and the South Atlantic. But the arbiter of this question, the International Hydrographic Organization (IHO), has decreed that though there were once four oceans there are now five, and only one Atlantic Ocean. In the spring of 2000, the IHO designated a fifth ocean on the planet. It carved out the Southern Ocean from the southern portions of the Atlantic, Pacific, and Indian oceans— basically all of the ocean below latitude 60° S. These are the waters surrounding Antarctica. As the oceans cover over 70 percent of the earth, these are probably facts worth teaching the children. Why do we call it Earth again?

Sailors have always known about the Southern Ocean, and have spoken of it as such, usually in hushed tones. These were the latitudes you had to visit to get around Cape Horn at the bottom of South America, or the other great capes of the world: Africa's Cape of Good Hope and Australia's Cape Leeuwin. And these were necessary voyages before the two great canals were cut across the Isthmus of Panama and the sands of Egypt. With the Southern Ocean waters girdling the planet, the seas can become fearsome. Sailors of old had a saying that below 50° S there is no law, and below 60° S there is no God.

The North Pole is a place at sea, frozen waters in the midst of the Arctic Ocean. No human being has ever seen the North Pole without a layer of pack ice, but many scientists believe that opportunity is coming. The fabled Northwest Passage is already ice free for some months of the year, and the Canadians, who claim sovereignty over this waterway, announced the first transit of a commercial vessel in 2008. The South Pole is of course a point on land, a coordinate on the continent of Antarctica; land surrounded by water, the opposite of the North Pole's geography.

It strikes me as amusing that in the same decade where we gained an ocean, we lost a planet. Pluto was reduced to the rank of an asteroid by the International Astronomical Union in 2006, but despite this demotion, the number of heavenly orbs in our solar system is still the same, and notwithstanding the elevated status of the Southern Ocean, there is not one extra drop of water in the world. It all sounds like relabeling without change, but labels guide our understanding and we should take heed of these things.

At sea, the oceans are immensely powerful. It is easy to believe that these seas lie far beyond the power and influence of mankind, but that is not the case. Along their many coasts they can die the death of a billion cuts—more, really, as over half the world's population lives within 60 miles of the coast. The oceans have many problems: drift-net fishing, endangered species, drillers, pollution, and always, the press of humanity. The list is long. Out here I feel a connection to these things that I don't feel at home or at the fish market, or I should say at a seafood restaurant, which is the closest I come to a fish market.

I sometimes wince for the oceans, and tossing trash over the side can trigger those thoughts, even if that trash is only food scraps and paper, which is all it ever is, the biodegradables that are allowed to be tossed. That is, apart from the flushing of the toilet. *Rubicon*, like most sailboats, is equipped with a holding tank for human waste. In coastal waters, the tank is used and periodically pumped out at dockside facilities. The holding tank strategy doesn't work on long offshore passages due to the size of the tank, and, more importantly, the necessity for them doesn't exist, so offshore, the toilet on a sailboat is flushed directly into the sea, which is a practical and ethical arrangement. The ocean can deal with a few pounds of human excrement, but it can't deal with plastic. It is illegal to dispose of plastic anywhere at sea, which is a good thing. If you know how long plastic takes to decompose you shouldn't need the law, but I'm glad it's there. The oceans are our lifeline to the future, but they enjoy few global protections.

Didn't I read somewhere that the food chain starts out here? The fragile health of our oceans presents an existential threat to the human race. It is too bad that they belong to everyone, and hence to no one. The oceans, or the high seas as we still think of them, are largely international waters, and they are the essence of planetary globalization. In fact, if we take out all those coastal waters where nations claim sovereignty, international waters still cover more than half of our planet. It's still pretty much anything goes on the high seas as we continue the shortsighted squandering of our inheritance. I used to think our biggest existential threat was nuclear Armageddon, but it seems that threat may have been averted. Nuclear weapons may be used in the years ahead, but it will likely be one or two, maybe a few. It will not be the massive exchange of warheads between empires that the world had feared. The world and our civilization will not end in a nuclear winter. I then thought global warming was the planet's biggest existential threat, but I'm bumping the warm-up down to the number two spot. I think number one belongs to the oceans. We probably can't kill them, but we can cripple them, and that would be a shame for our species.

It doesn't seem that many speak of duty anymore; the focus is more on rights and privileges. I remember the righteous joy I felt when I refused to write a letter for an employee asking the court to excuse him from jury duty on the grounds that he was vital to the company. I enjoyed telling him that his presence was not that crucial. The draft was over, all his country asked for were taxes and jury duty, but still he shirked. We have a duty to protect the oceans, but who thinks of them except as a means to material gain or recreation?

Now it's fog and rain, with light and fickle winds as we slowly escape the Gulf Stream. I'm more than a little ready to change this movie from *Singing in the Rain* to *Chariots of Fire*, but in the meantime I'll finish reading Bill Bryson's *The Lost Continent*. Whatever else is happening, that man can make you laugh.

THE RISK BUDGET

Every man has the right to risk
his own life in order to preserve it.
—JEAN-JACQUES ROUSSEAU

The rain has not let up all morning and my seaboots have finally soaked through. Scratch one pair of dry socks. After donning one of my few remaining pairs, I've slipped my feet into plastic grocery bags before pulling my boots back on. They're feeling quite toasty now.

While I had my socks off, I took a few minutes to examine my feet. Apart from being very pale and a tad shriveled, they look healthy enough. Out here you really need to inspect things constantly, moving about with your eyes open, inspecting as you go. The proverbial stitch in time may save the rig, or the entire project; sailing is risk management 101.

When I worked as a portfolio manager, and later as a nonportfolio manager, I gave a lot of thought to risk, a topic that gets plenty of airtime on Wall Street, but not always enough uncluttered consideration. You can't control risk until you understand what the risks really are, a process of identification and categorization, and what potential impact a realized risk might deliver, issues of measurement and estimation. Only then can you design and implement some controls.

Not too many years ago the term "risk budget" emerged as a buzzword in the investment business. Risk budgeting in the financial world is a multilayered process, the essence of which is to harness various tools, approaches, and measurements to manage the risk/return profile of an investment portfolio. Because changes in a given investor's risk appetite tend to occur slowly, much of the work involves researching, building, and balancing a portfolio of assets that can be expected to generate the highest returns for a specified level of risk. It could be well summed up by George Patton's dictum, "Take calculated risks. That is quite different from being rash." If one looks at it from the other side, as setting a return target and then structuring the portfolio likely to meet that target with the lowest risk profile, one can see the generality of the approach. This got me thinking that there are risk budgets in life as well as in portfolios. We see people depleting their risk budgets every day: smoking, driving recklessly, working in a field that is wrong for them, or staying with a person who is wrong for them; all high risks for questionable returns. I wanted the returns—the rewards—that would come from doing a solo transatlantic, but I wanted to minimize the risk profile.

When I took up solo sailing, I tried to identify the particular risks I would face. I opened my notebook and wrote "Ten Fears" at the top of the page, subconsciously substituting the word "fear" for "risk"—not exactly a synonym but close enough. At the end of the exercise I came up with only eight. Here is my list, in alphabetical order so I can avoid having to properly rank the unavailability issue: collision, falling overboard, fear itself, gear failure (particularly hull, rig, or rudder), injury or sickness, navigational errors, unavailability (for the kids), and weather.

For each risk factor, I developed a strategy to minimize the risk. Often it involved education, and hours were spent hitting the books on first aid, navigation, and weather systems. Sometimes the solution was defined by equipment and systems: life raft, AIS, EPIRB, and a few thousand dollars worth of et cetera. Discipline was also a critical strategy, such as the personal mandate to clip on when working on the foredeck. In practice of course, staying risk controlled was a blended strategy.

It is always possible that some random event can blow your risk budget—the nonsmoker attacked by lung cancer, or the chance meeting with a drunk driver—but random events can devastate budgets of all types. Shit happens, as they say. I like to budget. If you don't budget, how would you ever know when you were breaking the budget? Realistic budgets are excellent navigational tools in our universal passage.

I remember the week I announced my resignation from Brown Brothers, Harriman & Co., an old-line Wall Street firm (and by old-line I mean founded in 1818; U.S. businesses don't get much more old-line than that). They were set to celebrate their 175th year of operation when I left to join a start-up firm with no assets under management and no track record. Brown Brothers is a fine institution, and despite whatever brickbats are thrown at Wall Street these days, I'm proud to have worked there. During my last days at the firm, some of the other managers stopped by my desk to wish me well, and one said, "You've really got balls, man." What man wouldn't want to accept that line? The risk was in the future, and so for a few days I walked around feeling much taller than the 5'8" I stand in dress shoes. Unfortunately, it was all nonsense. The odds were pretty fair that we could make a go of it, but so what if we had failed? I wouldn't have been marched behind the building and shot. I would simply have had to find another job, and that was easier in those days than it might be today.

As thoughts of those days come back to me, the fog of memory clears, and so I must admit the truth. There were many sleepless nights before the decision to cast my lot with a start-up was made, so many in fact that my wife had relegated me to the sofa bed in our family room. Despite my temporary banishment, Gail's support was invaluable. She fortified me. I can only speak lightly of the risk now because of the strength I took from her in those pivotal days. The decision was made, the anxiety faded, and I returned to the bedroom.

We need to be suspicious when we look at the specials on the risk menu, but we can't skip all the entrees. We each choose our own risks, and then we pray for a little luck. I have an aversion to irrational risks. Consequently, I have totally rationalized my involvement with solo sailing and the OSTAR.

■ ■ ■

The afternoon has brought an end to the rain and a steady breeze has filled in from the south, perfect conditions for the genny. With the big sail set, we're on the move again and hopefully leaving the Gulf Stream behind. We should have been well clear by now, but we seem to have caught a foul current from the stream. We're fighting our way out, but the victory is slow in coming.

CONNECTIONS

*Tug on anything at all and you'll find it
connected to everything else in the universe.*

—JOHN MUIR

A t a time when I should be on dry land, shaving off my beard,
having a much-needed drink, and enjoying hearth and home,
I am still out here battling gear and the elements. Today's battle
was more than a little wearing. First light found *Rubicon* humming
along nicely under full main and genoa, close-hauled and spray
flying. We were doing a good turn of speed, whatever it was, but
the boat was on the cusp of being overpowered. It was time to roll
in some of the genny. I was about half done with this routine task
when the roller furler stopped, cold and frozen. I couldn't roll up
any more of the sail and I couldn't let it back out. (A roller furler
allows a headsail to be rolled up around the forestay like the old
window shades. It saves a huge amount of energy—particularly
with the larger headsails—compared to hank-on sails that are attached with special shackles called hanks. On the other hand, the
hanks rarely fail.) This was a serious situation; in fact, the most
serious issue I have faced so far. The big sail was halfway out, and
jammed, a definite problem if we're visited by another gale. Also,
in lighter winds and in order to get to Newport before the next
OSTAR, I need the genoa.

An examination convinced me that the furling line had become tangled in the furling drum, which is right at the bow of the boat, though how this might have happened was a mystery to me. There was no way to take a shortcut in untangling the line inside the drum. The drum has side openings for the line to enter, but if the line suddenly freed up while part of the sail was in a strong breeze, the rest of the sail would come exploding out, spinning the drum and ensuring that my piano playing days are over, and it's an instrument that I've always wanted to learn. So the first order of business was to lash the furling drum to prevent any rotation. I then removed the furling line, which runs through various guides from the bow back to the cockpit, and began the laborious task of unwinding and rewinding. I had already turned the boat downwind as it would have been an impossible job to accomplish while bouncing to windward on the bow of the boat.

So this morning's on-deck activity was sitting on the anchor roller at the forward tip of the boat and pulling about 50 feet of line through the drum. It was necessary to do this procedure twenty-five times to get it all out and then another twenty-five times to rewind it properly, all while the line seemed intent on diving into the water and generally getting in the way. The rain had stopped falling and I relished the great view of the ocean sliding under her bow as *Rubicon* pranced along. Coloring the negative side was my awareness of an approaching cloud bank and our distance clocked in the wrong direction. Finally the job was completed, the roller furler was back in action, and we were back on course. When I went below I was surprised that it was already past lunchtime, so I called my breakfast lunch and took a nap.

There is a fine satisfaction in having resolved the problem du jour, and for the moment I'm putting aside the question of how it happened in the first place. As I've admitted earlier, technical ability is not my strongest suit, but I've had a technical epiphany today. While working at the bow I realized that all of the serious equipment problems I've experienced on this passage are the result of one bad gasket. Here are the connections. The gasket that started it all is the one around the inspection plate on the starboard fuel tank. Because it disintegrated, small pieces of gasket material were floating around the tank and periodically blocking the fuel intake line for the generator. Because of the blocked fuel line, the generator would frequently shut down and be difficult to restart. Because of the generator problems, I turned to running the main engine in neutral to charge the boat's batteries. For reasons that are too boring—and too unflattering to me—I will skip the details in my thinking that led me to give the batteries less than a full daily charge. This, I now believe, allowed a cumulative deficit to develop, and when the heavier sea conditions put greater demands on the autopilot, it blew a fuse. (Who knew there was a fuse tucked in the control box?) Then, yet one more of the multitude of gaps in my knowledge of all things nautical caused me to misdiagnose the problem and conclude that rewiring the "SeaTalk bus" was the desired strategy. Because of the—we have to say incompetent— rewiring job, a small fire was started in the wiring behind the control panel, effectively knocking out the boat's instruments and autopilot for the duration. I haven't found the connection to the jammed furler yet, but no doubt it's there. For starters, we might well be in Newport now but for the aforementioned problems, and then whatever malevolence was lurking inside the furler could have surfaced after the race. Everything happens for a reason.

Actually, I've never cared for that old "everything happens for a reason" chestnut. Of course it's true, literally. They say the entire universe can be described by the laws of physics and chemistry. The reasons can be less granular, but they are always there. There is cause and effect, but I've long stopped believing some benevolent fellow is dealing out the deck and musing to himself that this card will help one of his little creations find his inner strength. Everything may happen for a reason, but when you hear it said you always know the line that will come next: "When one door closes, another door opens." Have you looked out some of those doors?

Speaking of everything happening for a reason, I've just made an entry in the log and I notice that we are passing 50 miles south of the RMS *Titanic*, now resting on the bottom of the Atlantic at

41° 46' N, 50° 14' W. She sank in 1912, almost a hundred years ago, but the timing that I think about is that she went down in mid-April and it is now late June. The risk from ice recedes as we move toward the summer months and I have few worries about ice on this passage.

Those competitors taking the more northerly route do have to keep an eye out for ice. Unfortunately, sometimes keeping an eye out isn't enough. A big iceberg might be hard to miss, but a growler—a chunk of ice barely visible above the waterline—would be easy to hit, and could slice a hole in the bottom of a sailboat with the ease of a can opener liberating a bowl of soup. The northerly route is tempting for the simple fact that it's shorter. It cannot accurately be described as the great circle route, which is the shortest, as that route would have you bumping into Newfoundland, but it's close. Fortunately, the history of the race provides a number of winners who have taken more southerly routes, and that was all the evidence I needed to give the ice some distance.

One of the positive results from the tragedy of the *Titanic* was the formation of the International Ice Patrol. With the exception of a few war years, the Ice Patrol has been in continuous operation since 1914. Its function is to develop and share information with mariners on the extent of the ice field, or what they refer to as "the limit of known ice." Now, of course, you can find their charts online.

We've tacked over to starboard, and we're sailing on a beam reach—the wind hitting the boat at a more or less perpendicular angle to our direction of travel. The wave heights are in the low teens, not particularly large for offshore, where the waves tend to spread out. With the waves arriving at a measured pace, rather than all bunched together, the boat can usually ride the waves rather than crashing into them or pounding off the wave tops. Tonight, however, the combination of the point of sail and the wave direction is making for an uncomfortable ride. Rain complements the rocky ride, but we're moving right along on the path to Newport. I've no complaints, though I am dining belowdecks tonight where I can take off my rain gear for a while. It's pasta night again, and I pull one of the small cans of lemonade out of the icebox to find it totally empty. Corrosion has formed a pinhole in the bottom of the can and the lemonade has all drained out. I check the remaining three cans and they're all empty, which for some reason makes me laugh, so I just put on the kettle for tea and settle in for the night.

LOSING THE GENOA

*I can conceive of no contentment of which
toil is not to be the immediate parent.*
—ANTHONY TROLLOPE

The sky is as blue as a child's drawing and the sun as welcome as
payday. It is perhaps the second day of the passage that really feels
like summer. The winds are light and the seas have settled down,
very much a repeat of last week's experience.

The only situation marring today, and it is a real disappointment,
is the roller furler. To my chagrin, in fact to my utter and complete
disgust, the furler has jammed again. Yesterday I was congratulating
myself for fixing this problem. Oh well, that was yesterday. Once
again I have spent the morning going through the same drill with
the furling line, but this time it didn't solve the problem, which
means that the problem was not with the furling line at all and I just
got lucky yesterday. Whatever the case, it's jammed full and well now,
but at least the genoa is all rolled in. I don't have any other ideas for
clearing the problem. Removing the entire unit for examination
would require securing the mast, as the furler is linked into the
forestay holding the mast forward. That would be a major job at sea,
and probably not a worthwhile exercise at this stage in the race. The
genoa, a powerful sail for the lighter airs, is out of commission.

To keep my spirits up I have done a major cleanup, starting
with washing my hair and ending with a good clear-out of the

fridge. It took me a while to toss all of the questionable items overboard. Toward the end I began to imagine some great sea creature surfacing to investigate the source of this bounty.

While I was clearing the galley I did another count of my apples. I've become very security conscious regarding the apples. I eat about two a day, which is odd as I probably average two a month at home, and I was rather ignoring the whole basket of them before it warmed up. Now they are the only fresh fruit I have left. They seem like a precious gift, and they trigger that little OCD gremlin that requires a count a few times every day.

The apples may be rationed, but there is no shortage of food aboard. Despite the fact that I've been at sea for almost four weeks, I still feel like I'm on a floating pantry. Before leaving Newport, Bill had suggested I do the provisioning with his friend Ginny, who had worked as a cook on an Atlantic passage. I didn't think this was really necessary. After all, I'd read a book on provisioning for long sea passages and I'd completed a few short ones to Bermuda. However, I sensed Bill's concern that we would get halfway to Plymouth and discover that the only food left in the galley was a box of Mallomars, so I told him to go ahead and make the arrangements.

Ginny was an attractive and enthusiastic young woman, and I quickly came to appreciate the wisdom of Bill's suggestion. She also had a membership card at one of the huge box stores where you can provision for a regiment, so we bought in bulk and I saved a nice bit of change. In addition to provisioning for a crew of three for the eastbound passage, we decided to also provision the nonperishables for the return passage to simplify matters in Plymouth. We pulled up to the checkout counter with bulging shopping carts, mini-trucks almost, the Humvees of the shopping cart world, and I enjoyed the puzzled look of the cashier as we transferred cartons and cases from the carts to the conveyor belt. I smiled and told the cashier that we had a really large family. Men can be such jerks sometimes.

I took a long nap this afternoon, made an early dinner, and with the winds settled down I took the opportunity to effect a proper repair of the solent. With the sail spread over the foredeck, hours were consumed sewing a large rectangular patch on the sail while trying not to include any body parts in the stitching. The sun slid over the horizon, painting the sky with a pastel palette as I attached the sail hanks to the inner forestay and winched the halyard tight. Once more *Rubicon* had a headsail flying. The repair took almost 3 hours, and it's not a pretty thing, but I'm confident the sail will hold till Newport.

The loss of the genoa is another setback in terms of my ETA in Newport, so expectations will have to be revised again. However, though I've lost the use of the genoa with the freezing up of the furling gear, my sail repair has put the solent sail back in the lineup. The solent is smaller than the genoa, but it's far bigger than the storm jib. It's a sail that can catch some wind.

We are doing a slow lope on a silvery evening in a waning wind. There is no doubt it's all good. Staring at the fruits of my labor, full and drawing, I munch my way through a sheaf of pretzel rods, holding them like cigars, while Etta James sings to me.

HITTING THE WALL

*When you get to the end of your
rope, tie a knot and hang on.*
—FRANKLIN D. ROOSEVELT

Today has been harsh. That is not a word I would use to describe any previous day of this passage, but this one well deserves the descriptive. It began well enough—in fact, the dawn was a beautiful bookend to last night's sunset, and I moved about the boat with enthusiasm and pride in our progress. Sailing is problem solving, and seeing the headsail strong against the morning sky was clear evidence of at least one problem solved.

With no pressing jobs on the boat, I made my favorite breakfast with lots of corned beef and the last of the eggs. With bread that still passed muster, if you didn't look too hard, and a large mug of coffee, it seemed a fine brunch, splendid actually as I drank in the beauty of sea, sky, and sails. We were slicing through the easy sea conditions with *Rubicon* gradually stepping it up as the wind freshened. Then the trouble began. As we came over one very modest wave, *Rubicon* began to round up into the wind, and I had to quickly release the wheel to bring us back on course. When Hydro is steering the boat, the main rudder is locked down, and therefore the wheel also. This is because the wind vane steers through a small auxiliary rudder attached to the back of the boat. I assumed that the sweet spot for the main rudder had shifted, and thought that once I'd reset the main rudder all would be well, so when I felt we were back in the groove I once again locked down the wheel. Unfortunately, the effort produced no improvement and we soon rounded up again. I made a quick examination of the self-steering gear, including a look down at the auxiliary rudder shaft bolted to the transom, but all I could see there was foaming water as we plunged along. With nothing visibly amiss, I gave Hydro a reprimand for dereliction of duty and continued as before.

Thus began a long morning of trimming the sails and adjusting the wheel and the vane in a futile courtship to bring my crucial companion back into the game. Perhaps it was denial, but it was a long time before I could accept the reality that Hydro, my invaluable crewmate, had abandoned her post. With this fact finally hammered home, I leaned over the transom and examined Hydro from top to bottom, and saw that the problem was indeed at the bottom. I could see the strut projecting just below the waterline, where it should have been attached to the auxiliary rudder. As the passing of a wave allowed the transom to lift into the air, I saw with horror that the auxiliary rudder was gone, now very obviously resting on the floor of the Atlantic. It had been out of sight and out of mind, and it was now out of action. Only yesterday I was bemoaning the loss of the genoa due to the jammed furler, but this was far worse. Every time something breaks on this boat, it's an item of more consequence than the one before. What's next, a problem with the mast or the main rudder? But no, I doubt that. Those items are integral parts of the boat, vital organs really, and the boat has never failed me. I was just having equipment problems, but this one was a nasty setback. A quick check of my handheld GPS showed that we were still 757 nautical miles from Newport, perhaps another five days of sailing and a long way to hand steer.

There was really no time to dwell on the disappointment. The wind and seas had both been building and I had taken in no sail, being preoccupied with the steering issue. I pointed *Rubicon* close to the wind, where it was easier for her to hold a course, quickly tied down the wheel and began the exercise. The first priority was to take a second reef in the main. In preparation for this I went to lower the traveler, which would ease the boom to leeward. As we were already sailing close-hauled, this would point the mainsail into the wind and make it easier to lower the sail to the reef point. The traveler lines are long enough that I can easily wrap them around a winch, which allows me to ease the traveler with only a modest tension on the line. Whatever passing thoughts clouded my judgment at that moment—no doubt some mixture of anger and frustration at Hydro's demise —the result was that instead of employing the winch, I simply grabbed the line and flipped it out of the line stopper. This left me woefully unprepared to control the line, and in the moment it took to relax my grip I was pulled off my feet. I fell hard and face down in the cockpit, my head just missing the coaming, the 4-inch sill separating the cockpit and the four-step companionway leading below. Pain now radiated from my right arm and knee. I remained lying in the cockpit for a few minutes collecting myself, and after some checking I realized with relief that the fall would leave behind only a few bruises. It was my first fall on the passage and I had been lucky, perhaps undeservedly as the tumble was brought on by my own carelessness. I would think of it as my wake-up fall. The day had taken quite a nosedive from its initial satisfactions and, as if to set the stage for the next act, low-level clouds had gradually filled in until the beautiful blueness of brunch was overtaken by ranks of somber grays. It was time to reengage, so I pulled myself up, secured a reef in the mainsail, and returned to the wheel.

I then ran below where I retrieved some bungee cords, a long spool of light line, and a bar of chocolate. Unless I could fashion some method of steering assistance, it would be a long slog to Newport. The boat would have to be hand steered, assisted by whatever cobbled-up system could do the job. There was now a third requirement to keeping a course without a helmsman. It was still vital to have the sails trimmed properly, and the rudder in the sweet spot, but now there needed to be just the right degree of tension applied to the wheel. Neither locking down the wheel nor giving it free rein would work. I tied small loops around the outside end of each spoke of the big wheel. I was then able to take a bungee and hook it quickly to the appropriate loop. To each bungee

I secured a length of light line and ran the line down through the pad eyes that were conveniently located on the cockpit bulkheads on either side of the wheel, and through small line clutches. I had installed the clutches back in Plymouth to help in locking down the wheel when using the Hydrovane and never imagined they would be such a crucial factor in my jury-rigged steering system. By adjusting the lines—more or less bungee and more or less line—I could dial in the tension to each side of the wheel, and it was as much the relative tensions of the lines as the absolute tension that dictated success or failure. It was a tedious job and required frequent resetting. Too much tension on the windward side, and the boat would round up into the wind; too little and we would bear off downwind.

The wind was now up, blowing hard from the southwest, and the waves were building. It was time to tuck the third reef in the main and reef the solent. If Hydro had still been on the job, I would have been comfortable with only the second reef, but with conditions deteriorating I opted for the security of the third reef. As I lowered the main I received one more of the rude shocks that were punctuating this day. Instead of dropping neatly over the boom, all of the mainsail, except the sail area above the third reef point, which was held aloft by the main halyard, slid off the sail track on the mast and splayed all over the deck. Whatever the cause of this latest problem, my immediate concern was to limit any damage that might be done with eight metal sail cars banging around on the deck. I grabbed a coil of spare line and made my way to the mast, where I clipped in and held on while lashing the sail as tightly as possible to the boom. My energy was fading with the light, so I repaired to the galley for the comfort of food. After smearing generous quantities of peanut butter on some biscuits, I forced myself to drink two cups of water. This day was unfolding much more aerobically than planned, and dehydration can arrive quickly out here.

The solent still needed a reef tied in, so I went forward to drop the sail, and then moved to the bow to put a line through the head of the sail and secure the flogging fabric while I tied in the reef points. As I grabbed the head of the sail, the shackle holding the halyard to the solent sail disengaged and flew up the mast. As God is my witness, I don't know how it got away from me. The halyard is a line that runs up the inside of the mast, exits past a block (pulley) at the top, and then comes back down to deck level where it can be attached to the head of a sail. When a halyard "escapes," two forces begin a little dance. The free end is lifted up by the wind and the speed of the boat, while the weight of the line inside the mast exerts its downward pull. Sometimes this dance ends before the swearing has quieted down, and sometimes not, but on anything but a calm day at the dock it is likely to end with the halyard's shackle jammed into the hardware at the top of the mast, and that is precisely what happened in this case. It is a royal inconvenience, as the only way to get your hands on the business end of the line is to climb the mast. I can't repeat the obscenities that I wanted to scream, but the swearing remained silent. Too exhausted to swear, and in a bit of a shock from the day's train of setbacks, I simply sat on the foredeck, staring up at the halyard as the spray dripped off my foulies. Finally, deflated and disgusted, I lashed down the solent and made my way back to the cockpit, where I hand steered until fatigue and frustration called a halt to the day's progress.

Rubicon could make little speed with no headsail and only a triple-reefed main, but it was now dark and I was approaching exhaustion, so I decided, for the first time on this passage, to heave-to. This is a way to set rudder against sail area such that the boat is essentially parked with the sails up. I then went below, where I started the engine to charge the batteries. Yet another routine procedure on the most nonroutine of days, and I should have expected disappointment. Almost immediately after starting, the engine began to cough and cut out, and I spent 10 minutes with one arm holding up the companionway steps while I frantically pumped the engine's manual fuel pump. Finally the offending air was cleared from the system and the engine roared back to life, assuming the only mission allowed it in the race, shepherding electrons into the boat's battery bank.

I threw a can of baked beans into a pot, warmed them quickly, and dumped them over two slices of bread. It was as much of a dinner as I could muster, and welcome fare it was. As I slowly packed away the beans I grew despondent over the many problems that accompanied the day's meager progress. For the first time, I allowed myself to consider the question of whether I would make it to Newport rather than when. With no steering assistance, and for the moment very little sail area, the remaining miles to Newport appeared more like the start of a second career than a sprint to the finish.

I've known a few fears on this passage, and I must admit that the emotion stopped by for a little visit before my hot bean dinner, but I'm fairly confident there will be no panic on the good ship *Rubicon*. I tripped the panic button once and found it to be the most useless of human behaviors. The panic button is like a malicious circuit breaker; just when you need to be focusing on some critical situation, it disables you.

It was a long time ago, during the first months of my marine training, and it was the day of the gas chamber exercise. We had our gas masks tightly secured as we were led into the old Quonset hut that was filled with some type of tear gas. The drill instructors also had their masks on, but theirs would be staying on. The exercise began with the order to remove our masks and sing the Marine Corps Hymn. Thank God it was just the first verse. After that croaky rendition, a drill instructor would work his way down the line and eventually stop in front of you. When he did, you were required to give your name, rank, and serial number. Then, and only then, could you head for the door.

Unfortunately, I hadn't even reached "the shores of Tripoli" before the gas was clawing its way up my nose and into my eyes and down my throat. All I could think of was getting out of that hellhole, and I started to scream and pound on the wall. Normally, the drill instructors would be all over me if I even allowed my eyes to wander as we marched our way through the days; they called it eyeballing, and it was a punishable offense. That afternoon, however, they could not have been less interested in my antics. My madness faded as the few gray cells that were still functioning did a little processing. There was clearly only one route to the sunlight; deliver the goods. A short while later I joined my comrades on the outside as we coughed away the gas, wiped the snot from our running noses, and splashed water in our eyes. Not an activity I would care to repeat, but another great lesson generously given by the U.S. Marine Corps. I had learned the lunacy of hitting the panic button. I don't understand why we even have these things.

After making a last entry in the log, I remove my harness and stretch out on my sea berth. Despite my ramblings about a controlled situation, I can sense that my emotions are getting ready to stage a coup and start controlling events, so I quickly counterattack by falling into a sound sleep. I wake just as the blackness is receding. The plotters are gone.

COMPASS AWARENESS

*It was the forty-fathom slumber
that clears the soul and eye and heart,
and sends you to breakfast ravening.*
—RUDYARD KIPLING

M om was right; things do look better in the morning.
I woke from a few hours of sleep with a steely determination. As I sit holding that first vital cup of tea and waiting
for my morning oatmeal to cool, I hear myself issue the order, my
command voice saying, "*Rubicon*, you and I will sail into Newport
Harbor. We may be late, but we will sail in and preserve our
reputation." Perhaps it's silly, but saying it aloud seems to cement
the deal.

No doubt a part of my determination to sail into Newport
comes from the fact that I have no hull insurance on *Rubicon*. Not
that the current situation is desperate, but if yesterday's cascade
of calamities becomes a pattern, then the outlook could start to
look a little grim. All of the OSTAR competitors carry liability
insurance, but if you can avoid bumping into one of the other
boats at the start of the race, it's likely that your liability policy will
gather dust until expiration. Nevertheless, the policies are required,
expensive, and no doubt profitable to the insurance carriers.
Hull insurance is another matter. That coverage, essentially the
equivalent of collision insurance on your car, will pay for repairs

or replace your boat if lost at sea. It used to be an available option for singlehanders, but those days are gone. Most if not all of the sailors in this race are sailing without that comfort. To lose *Rubicon* out here would be a financial reverse that I would rather not contemplate, but to lose her at all would be hard. There would be guilt to expunge.

We lay hove-to through the night. Parking the boat is a simple affair. With the triple-reefed main sheeted in tightly and the traveler down, I come up extremely close to the wind, lose all forward momentum, and then turn the wheel hard over as if to tack. Of course, without any way on, the boat is unable to turn through the wind. The tack stalls and the boat simply sits. I then lash down the wheel and we're done. However, it seems that without a headsail—which would be "back-winded" in this maneuver, thus leaving the rig balanced and the boat stalled—*Rubicon* gets pounded a lot more, which I suspect might be stressing the large rudder. In fact, without a headsail we're not properly hove-to, but we are safe. The movement down below is jerky and unpredictable, so moving about requires even more care than usual, but that is a small thing. The big thing is the rudder. Will it hold? Right now I have to risk it as I don't see any alternative, but it worries me.

We're back in gale conditions, or just shy of them, but we need to get back to sailing. Dressing is a simple matter of slipping into my harness as the foul-weather gear and seaboots have stayed on. I untie the wheel, jibe around, and we're off. Despite the reduced sail wardrobe, *Rubicon* is moving quickly. Much of our progress appears to be up and down as we make our way over a tall wave train, but we're voyaging.

Hand steering in heavy weather is exhausting, but I determine to do 2-hour stints between breaks. About 90 minutes into this plan, a large wave slaps *Rubicon* on her starboard side; water quickly invades the cockpit and just as rapidly retreats out the open transom as we are slewed into a near broach (where the boat would get caught sideways to the waves). A shot of adrenaline lifts the fatigue from my arms and an "oh shit" escapes my lips, but it is the small "oh shit," the one demanding action, rather than the large "OH SHIT!" asking what can be done and soliciting resignation. I take a quick look at the compass and guide *Rubicon* back to her safety course, which at the moment is a course of 270°, due west.

Reliance on the compass and awareness of the safety course are elemental concepts of sailing, but it is easy to forget the basics when your situation is well camouflaged by winds, waves, or whatever.

I learned the necessity of compass dominance some years ago while crewing on a sailboat delivery from Annapolis to Virgin Gorda in the British Virgin Islands. It was late in the afternoon of day eight and we were running downwind in very respectable 12- to 15-foot waves. The boat, a fast 46-footer made by X-Yachts of Denmark, had a crew of five and we were doing a lot of hand steering. The delivery skipper had explained that this would be good practice for the crew, which it was, but it also gave some assurance that he would deliver the boat to her owners with a fully functioning autopilot since we never used it. It was late afternoon and a heavy overcast covered the sky. After taking the helm about an hour earlier, I was a picture of concentration as we flew down the waves making a solid 9 to 10 knots. My eyes darted from the wind instruments to the sails, then over my shoulder to note the next oncoming wave, and then back to the wind instruments. I was keeping her in the groove, loving it all and feeling confident of my skills when, in the time it takes to brew a cup of tea, my world changed. Darkness can fall quickly at sea, especially with clouds blanketing the sky, and just as the light was fading the rain was coming on, one of those steady drizzles that at our speed felt like a driving rain. And then, as I should have expected, came the wind shift.

Having focused solely on the visual course through the immediate wave neighborhood, and keeping the boat in that wonderful groove, I had stopped thinking about the compass. The boat was on a rail headed southeast, but when it all hit the fan I forgot I had a compass. After a bit of very unseamanlike banging around, I had the boat steadied and on the same point of sail with respect to the wind, but I had yet to adjust the sails and guide her toward the best course we could sail in the new wind conditions. My self-satisfaction was gone, and then my severely deflated ego received the coup de grace when the skipper yelled up the companionway, "Where ya going? We're headed back to Annapolis!"

Wind shifts can deal you a whole new hand, but you can't play the hand without looking at the compass. Never again would I stand at the helm without locking two numbers in my mind, the desired course and the safety course, and never again without compass awareness. When sailing deep downwind, where an accidental jibe is always a threat, my safety course would be 10 or 15 degrees higher than the desired course. If a wave, or a lapse in concentration, put us in danger of an accidental jibe, I would aim for the safety course until I could stabilize the situation and return to the true course. Of all the lessons I've learned over the years, from better sailors than I and from my own mistakes, this has been the most valuable, and the lesson is equally powerful on land.

I take a break to down a can of tuna and some crackers, and make a few notes in the log. My log entry reads, "Happy Birthday Steven, I wish I was with you." As a twenty-five-day passage had been my goal and my expectation, I had planned to see Steven on his twenty-third birthday, or at least call him from Newport and wish him well. I consider using the sat phone to give him a call, but I'm very preoccupied with the current situation, and I don't want any uncertainty to show in my voice, so I postpone that joy.

As the day grinds on, the sun is coming out and it's noticeably warmer. The waves are starting to settle but are still full of piss and vinegar, and it is very difficult to get the boat to steer herself in these conditions. I take another stint at the wheel, and steer out of another near broach during the third hour.

It may be all of the calories I've burned today, but I can't resist the idea of a hot and hearty meal, so I bring out the large pressure cooker I bought on eBay. It has turned into a valuable appliance and will be the perfect size for my mulligan stew. After rummaging through the food stores, I have assembled cans of chicken, green peas, corn, tomato sauce, and stewed tomatoes. There are still a couple of fresh potatoes left, and some onions. After cutting and boiling the potatoes, I add all my ingredients, throw in a handful of seasonings from the spice cabinet, and set the pot to simmer.

The pot is secured with a pair of Vise-Grips locked behind it, wedging it against the adjustable pot-holding arms on the stove. This arrangement never fails regardless of how much rock and roll is going on outside.

I had been spoiled with a series of excellent dinners on the eastbound passage. We were three days out of Newport when Bill and I discovered that Mike, a patent attorney and a very competent sailor, had another talent up his sleeve. I suppose it wasn't exactly a discovery. After one rotation in the galley, Mike asked us if we would mind if he cooked the dinners going forward. Bill and I looked at each other like we'd won the lottery. From then on we never missed a sit-down dinner. I even used the placemats. It was a time for conversation as well as nourishment, and it brought us closer together as a crew. Just before leaving the boat in Plymouth, Mike told me that he had made a short list of food items that I might want to resupply before the return passage. After he left, I took a look at his list and found that he had written cumin, along with a few more basic items. I was fairly sure I had never used cumin in my life, and wouldn't have been able to pick it out of a spice lineup, but I kept the list for a while as a reminder of the proper approach to a transatlantic passage.

It is late in the day and we've just passed longitude 56° W. Every meridian of longitude is a falling domino on the way home. We had just passed 54° W when Hydro died, so there is progress. There will be no balanced sail plan without a headsail, and there is no way I am climbing the mast under the current conditions, so it will be another night like last night, but with a dash more optimism. We are fighting our way west, there is a large pot of hot stew, and it all seems doable.

The stew is delicious and I eagerly fill a second bowl with the steaming concoction. The route from Plymouth to Newport is generally an upwind path. It's not particularly comfortable sailing, but it is easier for most boats to hold an unassisted course when going upwind. With a little help from my string and bungee arrangements, *Rubicon* is holding a decent course. The prospect of a competitive finish is dead, but there is still a passage to complete, a port to be made. Right now, however, there is only so much I can do topside, and there is nothing further that needs doing below, so I rest for a bit, comfortably tucked into the nav seat, one hand clutching my bowl, eating slowly and losing myself in the heat of the American Midwest. In his cleverly titled *I'm a Stranger Here Myself*, Bill Bryson is taking me on a road trip back to his roots in middle America.

BACK IN GEAR

It is only with the heart that one can see rightly;
what is essential is invisible to the eye.

—ANTOINE DE SAINT EXUPERY

As usual, I wake with a determination, which the day will no doubt whittle away. The first order of business is to get a headsail flying. I have been contemplating a climb up the mast to retrieve the errant solent halyard, but it is a chore I'm very unenthusiastic about. The truth of it is that I'm never enthusiastic to climb that aluminum stick—at 65 feet the height of a six-story building—and the top of it is now swinging an arc from wind and waves. I have climbed the mast before, many times in fact, for I have worked hard to meet this particular fear, but those climbs have always been with *Rubicon* comfortably nestled at the dock or resting on her mooring, not doing a three-dimensional square dance in the North Atlantic. I use my Topclimber, an ingenious piece of kit that is part harness and part climbing apparatus. It's harder work than being winched up by a crewmate, but the extra effort is a minor thing. What scares me now, beyond the usual, is the fact that the stability of a steady course can no longer be assumed, and I really don't want to be observing any drama from my aerial perch.

After the morning tea ritual I go on deck with my binoculars, move to the bow of the boat, and take a good look up the mast. The shackle at the end of the solent halyard is clearly visible, stuck in the block at the top of the mast. There are two headsail halyards on *Rubicon*; one is holding up the large genoa on the jammed roller furler, and the second is at the top of the mast. I am crouched on the foredeck and growing tired of waiting for the seas to calm down, or my courage to well up, when I have a major "duh" moment. There is no reason why one of the two spinnaker halyards could not do the job, and so I shackle one on, unlash the solent, tie in the reef, and hoist her up. The line runs fair and we accelerate as the small sail adds thrust to the project. Perhaps I'm not that sharp after almost a month at sea, or perhaps I'm just not that sharp, but I'm blaming this oversight on my preoccupation with the steering issue.

My next target is the mainsail, most of which is still lashed to the boom. An examination of the main reveals that the stopper bolt near the lower end of the mast track has worked loose and slid to the very bottom of the track. It's designed to be able to do this to allow the mainsail to be removed, and that is exactly what had happened. I move the halyard to a winch at the mast. From there I can work the mainsail back up, feeding a sail car into the track every few feet. Conditions still call for at least one reef, but it's necessary to pull the sail to its full height in order to secure the stopper bolt. I give thanks to whoever designed this little piece of gear for requiring that the stopper bolt be held captive. It could be loosened but not removed from the track, and this critical feature of its design has prevented it from bouncing into the sea. The average depth of the Atlantic is over 12,000 feet; I wonder how long it would have taken this vital little cog to find a resting place on the bottom.

Now we're looking more like a sailboat! The wind is moderating and is now down to the high teens, so we no longer need even the one reef, but I'm leaving it in as a smaller sail plan should make my bungee and string approach to course-keeping a tad more effective.

I know that I am losing weight, even though I seem to be grabbing a snack on half my trips belowdecks. Most of my preferred items are gone. There is no more fresh fruit, except for four tired apples, no more fresh anything actually, no more eggs, and only one bar of chocolate, but after a quick inventory through the various lockers I know that the last thing I have to worry about is running out of food. I will ration the remaining treats and work my way through the stacks of tuna cans. About a month before the OSTAR, I bought a case of MREs (Meals Ready to Eat), the same as those used by the U.S. military. They seemed like a good backup for the trip and I actually cooked one up the day they arrived. It was pure curiosity. I wanted to see how they compared with the old C-rations of my youth, or at least to my recollection of those rations. Better, but not great, was the verdict. However, they are great in the convenience area. You can forget about them for a year, then throw the foil pack in boiling water for a few minutes and your entree is ready.

At dawn we were hove-to, with no headsail flying and most of the mainsail out of action. Now we are sailing with a proper sail plan, and I am back to steering and tinkering with control lines. The assisted steering is working after a fashion. Much of the improvement comes from the moderation in wind and waves, but it is certainly helped by the addition of a headsail, and we are going in the right general direction. The cockpit is squared away with all the lines organized. It has been a good day's work and a satisfying day at sea.

With *Rubicon* taking care of herself for a little bit, I bat out a couple of quick e-mails, send them through my sat phone into the ether, and pick up any mail waiting for me on some distant server. It was a large e-mail catch this morning: Steven saying he'd enjoyed a fine birthday celebration, Amy announcing her school progress, and Barbara reporting that her lovely daughter gave her a third grandchild yesterday. It was another occasion I had more or less expected to be home for, but the important thing, as they always say and as it always is, is that the baby is healthy. He was born on Steven's birthday, a nice coincidence and another bond in my latest family. I can't wait to meet him.

The incoming e-mails also brought more somber news. Gianfranco Tortolani, one of the four Italians in the race, capsized during yesterday's gale. Apparently his boat was too badly damaged to be sailed into port, but it didn't sink and he was able to await rescue on the boat. After setting off his EPIRB, and no doubt spending some miserable hours rocking about on his wrecked boat, a freighter picked him up. He is bruised and his battered boat is lost, abandoned roughly 260 miles from the port city of Halifax, Nova Scotia, and about 200 miles ahead of me. I don't know if his boat will sink of its own accord, or if Gianfranco opened a seacock to ensure that it will soon slip below the waves, or if perhaps it will one day wash up on the coast of North America. The law of the sea commands that any boat or ship must divert to the assistance of a vessel in distress. Gianfranco is now on his way to wherever the freighter that came to his rescue is headed. It gives me perspective. I'm not the only one having problems, and I take a few moments to feel some gratitude for my current situation.

Thirty-one boats crossed the start line in this race; six have turned back after suffering various equipment issues, and now one is lost. At the start there were sailors from eight countries (United Kingdom-16, Italy-4, Netherlands-4, France-3, Austria-1, Germany-1, Ireland-1, United States-1—see Appendix). Twenty-seven men and four women, they are as varied a group of sailors and boats as could be found anywhere, with ages ranging from barely old enough to order a beer to comfortably into the grandparenting years. I had expected at least a few of my fellow countrymen to be competing, and at one time there had been five U.S. skippers with plans to make the start, but it is tough to make a May start line in England unless you bring your boat over the previous year, or have a very chilly transatlantic shakedown cruise just before the race. U.S. economic conditions have also made 2009 a very difficult time to break away for a long-distance yacht race.

Before heading east across the pond, I considered canceling. It seemed vaguely inappropriate to be engaged in such a personal, and in some ways selfish, endeavor while the country was suffering its current afflictions. However, well, here I am. Before leaving the States I did send an e-mail to the president's chief economic advisor with a few ideas. No doubt those remedies have been securely filed in his spam folder.

The Royal Western Yacht Club, the sponsor of the race, put out a very nice prerace program. It included pictures of each of the skippers and their boats and a half-page biography of each competitor. It was a little intimidating to read some of these bios, such as these comments on Pip Hildesly: "Pip took to the water as a toddler . . . Qualified as a yacht master instructor . . . and made a non-stop singlehanded return trip from Uruguay to the UK to get to the start line." Yikes!

The youngest competitor, Oscar Mead, not yet twenty and the youngest sailor to have ever qualified for the OSTAR, sailed many races as a teen with his father, and with a boat more toward the racing than cruising end of the spectrum, he looks to be a formidable competitor. One of the oldest in the race, Peter Crowther, is the landlord of a wonderful old establishment called the Green Dragon Pub. His bio reveals that this race is his eighth OSTAR, including one when his boat sank. That's pretty impressive for a race that's only held every four years. Yikes again!

The one commonality among the bios appears to be the early age at which they learned to sail and their lifelong connections to sailing. One of the bios, Katie Miller's, states that she "didn't start sailing until she was 12 years old," as if that was rather old to be taking up the sport. I feel outclassed and indeed I am, but no matter, I'll no doubt be a better sailor at the end of this enterprise than the start.

The OSTAR is a race for amateurs, and the main reward in their sights is the sheer thrill of crossing an ocean on their own boat and under sail. However, they are a competitive lot and hopes abound, particularly among a few of the younger competitors, who are using the race to gain enough experience and recognition to launch a sailing career. Sailing, and singlehanded sailing in particular, is a much bigger sport in Europe than it is in the United States. The finish of the last Vendée Globe around-the-world race saw thousands of people clogging the docks in Les Sables d'Olonne in southern France to welcome the winner, and French television provided extended live coverage. Of course it did help that the winner, Michael Desjoyeaux, was French.

The sun, wherever it is in this gray sky, is going down. The weather charts suggest that conditions could be a little uglier tomorrow, but with the rig sorted out I feel good about the situation.

I think of the lullaby I used to sing to Amy when she was a little girl, the one Bing Crosby sang in *White Christmas*. My crooning was pretty mediocre, but Amy seemed to like the old Irving Berlin song, "Count Your Blessings Instead of Sheep," and I did indeed fall asleep counting my blessings.

SINGING AT
THE HELM

Let me tell you the secret that has led me to my goal.
My strength lies solely in my tenacity.

—LOUIS PASTEUR

I was up three times during the night with the sails aback (a.k.a. back-winded, with the wind on the wrong side of the sail), and *Rubicon* headed back to England. It is incredibly frustrating, but I know I'm not the first sailor to fight this kind of battle. In fact, I am comforted by the knowledge that once again I can claim a common experience with Sir Francis Chichester. In addition to being a founding father of the OSTAR race, he was knighted by the queen at the age of sixty-five for his solo circumnavigation—the first such solo voyage by way of the old clipper route past the great capes. He describes this same affliction in his book *Gipsy Moth Circles the World*. Chichester had a wind-vane self-steering system, but it was a one-off, a version 1.0 in today's terms. Now these systems are well-tested products and invaluable, unless you happen to lose any critical bits, and then you are back on the same ocean, fighting the same battle as Sir Francis. He wrote, "At the time I thought it would drive me barmy but I kept at it day after day, trying every way I could think of to make it work. The self-steering performance slowly improved as time went by."

As I lie on my mat, I can feel *Rubicon* powering along, quick and steady; the only question is the course. My mind wants the answer to this rather fundamental question, but my body wants no part of the plan. My limbs feel heavy and slow to respond to instruction, but every mile in the wrong direction requires an additional mile the right way just to get back to here, and all the while I am aging and my boat is wearying. It is this simple and torturous arithmetic that gives me the strength to throw off my blanket, and the day is engaged.

Perhaps it's not such a bad thing that the off-course alarm is out of action. It might have been such a constant heckler that I would have taken a hammer to it. However, it wouldn't have been able to say much this morning, as we are actually headed in the right direction, give or take a few degrees.

My system of string and bungees hardly merits being labeled a steering system. It might more accurately be called a rudder moderation system. It starts with the main control lines on either side of the wheel, each with a bungee section that can be hooked to any particular lashed loop on the wheel, and a light line section going through a clutch. In heavy weather, additional lines are attached to keep the wheel from doing a 360° revolution. Although the wheel can turn two and a half times lock to lock, a full turn with the lines attached yields a tangled mess, and always requires "operator intervention." Right now it looks more like a cat's cradle because it's blowing hard on rough waters, and the wheel needs some extra lines to keep its movements in check.

With enough lines of the proper tensions, a phantom helmsman can be rigged. Not a very good helmsman to be sure, and an utter failure when sea or wind conditions change, or with the wind from behind, but certainly better than nothing. In heavy weather, there are more lines on the wheel than there are in the organization chart for the Pentagon, but it can usually be coaxed to hold a course long enough for me to grab a quick meal or a short nap. The days of experimentation have yielded some slight improvement, but I have to accept that this may be as good as it gets on the steering front. There is no magic system of strings that can duplicate what an autopilot or a wind vane or a human being can bring to the task. There are just too many variables: sail wardrobe, sail trim, sea conditions, wind direction, wind speed, and—not incidentally—the desired course you're trying to maintain. With all the variables, and the multiple settings for each one, I'm reminded of those formulas for combinations and permutations that I learned in college. It is simply a matter of experimentation, of endless trial and error.

I have taken to singing during these countless hours at the wheel, and where else can I sing as loudly as I like for as long as I like? Mostly I sing softly though. I've run through my repertoire many times. "Me and Bobby McGee" is a much-requested tune, and seems appropriate to the circumstances. Sometimes I sing to music playing from the speakers, but since I neglected to load up an iPod for the trip, and I can't keep running below to swap CDs, I mostly sing without electronic accompaniment, which also seems appropriate for this passage. And always, as fatigue sets in, I do my best rendition of "Sweet Chariot." This was another favorite of Amy's when I used to sing her to sleep, and it's one of the few where I remember all the words. "If you get there before I do, just tell my friends I'm a'comin' too. . . ."

A sharp squall is passing through. I'm standing at the helm in my heavy-weather stance—legs braced, arms and hands working the big wheel, and my head swiveling between rig, waves, and compass. Fatigue is migrating from my arms through the rest of my body, and that weariness has led to another near broach, which some aggressive steering has just left behind. I am bareheaded when I glance down to check the compass heading, as I have done many times already in this latest trick at the wheel. Just as my eyes leave the compass I catch sight of my reflection in the darkened screen of the inert chartplotter. My hair is combed straight back by the wind, quite different from the style I've affected since I started shaving. "Holy shit, I'm going bald," I shout. In the time it takes a wave to pass under the hull my whole focus has gone from seamanship to vanity, and I can't leave it behind until a thorough examination of the new defollicalized zone, the DFZ, has been made. I doubt that it has changed much in the past year, but it has always been easy to ignore on land where I shower without mirrors and comb quickly. Who knew that vanity had such power?

I'm starting to feel more and more like Dorothy trying to find her way home from Oz. Perhaps I feel this way because it was two months ago today that we cast off the dock lines and sailed out of Narragansett Bay bound for England. It's a lot of time to spend on a boat, and a long time at sea. In any event, I don't have a yellow brick road, just meridians of longitude. The second of two nasty squalls has just blown through, the clock hand is ticking past midnight, and we are crossing 60° W—how satisfying that is, particularly as I lost Hydro back at 54° W. Plymouth is located at approximately longitude 4° W and Newport just past 71° W, so that's the line. We're not in home waters yet, but now the bailout options are Martha's Vineyard or Nantucket instead of the Azores. I've found myself thinking about the next OSTAR, which probably means that I've been out here too long. Nevertheless, the thought is slowly germinating that, God willing, there will be a next OSTAR for me.

Why would I want to do another OSTAR? I'd better answer that question before committing any focus, or any other resources, to a "next time." Right now, the only answers that jump to mind are redemption, fun, and, if the stars align, a split second of glory. For better or worse, those rewards are not lacking in attraction, but I wonder how compelling I should allow them to be. I suppose I'd like to have a do-over, a chance to do the race with all systems go. There aren't many do-overs in the adult world, except with games. There will always be next year's big game, or in the case of the OSTAR, the big game four years down the road.

It's the old cartographic conundrum over where to draw the line between self-actualization and self-absorption, between expression and escape. Young people are often advised to follow their passion, and it's good advice, but you can't leave it there. Carpe diem indeed. I think it best to put these thoughts on the shelf for now. I still have this OSTAR to complete.

Some say that life isn't a race, but of course there are many times when you need to find a competitive edge. "All's fair in love and war," as the saying goes, but beyond these arenas of lethal combat there are times in your passage when you need to go for it. However, I think you can lose something precious if you view everything through the prism of winners and losers, and consequently I've changed my outlook on this OSTAR. Fortunately, my new perspective properly reflects my awareness that I won't be a part of the first group, and my reluctance to consider myself among the second. Be that as it may, it is now a passage, a rare opportunity and a great treat. Of course, I do have to make it to Newport by the fifth of July. That is the deadline for official finishers, and passage or race, I'll be damned if *Rubicon* and I will be denied that honor.

An e-mail arrives from Kevin, my friend and sailing mentor, who has been following the race closely. He's learned that the *Maersk Missouri* is the ship that rescued Gianfranco, and that the ship is destined for Port Newark in New Jersey, a half-hour drive from Kevin's house. What are the odds? Being the seaman that he is, Kevin has arranged to meet Gianfranco when the ship docks and help him get sorted out.

Dinner is a can of chicken curry, and despite the grading on a curve that often applies to passage food, the meal is very forgettable. I try to redeem it with a mug of tea and the dregs from the cookie tin, most of which are as forgettable as the dinner. Today seems like a long day, but they're all long now.

SAILING OFF
THE CALENDAR

In civilized life, law floats in a sea of ethics.

—EARL WARREN

Yet again I wake to find the sails aback and this time we have lost more than 8 minutes of longitude, more miles in the wrong direction. My inclination is to run topside to square things away but I refrain; the boat is safe and stable and I am neither. I am exhausted and still fogged with sleep; best to take a few minutes and pull myself together.

On deck I clip in right away as the seas are already 7 to 10 feet, and it is clear that another damn squall is bearing down. I'm guessing that it's blowing in the high 20s, with more wind coming. *Rubicon* is wearing her standard battle dress. Two squalls come through with barely enough time to hit the head (a.k.a. bathroom) between them. At noon I fire up the small GPS unit to find that our distance to go has just dropped below 500 miles. It feels like a victory. We have now covered a third of the distance that remained when I lost Hydro, and any question of bailing out has long been banished, though it was fairly academic as there are few bailout options from here. The truth is that it was rotten luck to lose Hydro. I would scream foul, but the sea has no referees.

By late afternoon the seas have calmed down and *Rubicon* is sailing well on my string and bungee system. Sailors typically name their self-steering systems, and it strikes me that I should name Hydro's replacement. Of course, it's not really a self-steering system, but even with all its limitations it keeps us sailing more often than not when I'm away from the helm. It is also evolving to meet new conditions, and it is teaching me a few tricks about sail trim and balance, so for all that it deserves a name. Unfortunately, I'm tired and the best I can come up with is Juribass, an acronym for jury-rigged bungee and string system. It also suggests that the jury is still out on the bastard. I have clearly been spending too much time by myself!

I've had the pleasure of steering all day, a long and wet march, but not as rough as yesterday. I know that all these hours at the helm have been a gift. They've been exhausting, and the number has brought some tedium, but there is a joy in driving *Rubicon*. At the helm I feel very much the captain, and I savor the feeling of commanding this beautiful vessel. Despite the satisfactions, right now my arms feel like lead and my shoulders ache; I take a couple of Motrin as I head below to spend an hour writing up my trip notes and considering dinner.

There is no longer much time for reading, but in those moments when I'm not hand steering or tinkering with Juribass I still reach for a book. Paul Krugman's *The Return of Depression Economics and the Crisis of 2008* has just been returned to the shelf. It was my second reading of his compelling little book. He includes a lot of financial history, and for some reason I want to lock in those facts. It was one of the many "serious" books I stowed for the trip, though many have remained unopened. I have been drawn mostly to fiction on this voyage, and that strikes me as proper. We need to read nonfiction for facts, but we read fiction for truths, and I suppose I've been looking for a few truths out here. Pretty soon I will be back on land, trying to get my arms around lots of new facts, some of them true.

Just before I committed to doing the OSTAR, a decision prompted by three parts romanticism and one part scotch, I paused to ask myself if this was a good time to be going off on a sailing adventure, with the world seemingly going to hell in a handbasket. It had been pretty clear that dark clouds were forming over the financial markets and the economy as we went into 2008. Sitting in my home in New Jersey, I didn't have access to the river of market data and analysis that flows daily into an investment firm. I was less connected to the thinking of the fine minds on Wall Street, and there are many brilliant minds there, but I was also without any incentive to put a more optimistic spin on the economic situation, a perennial problem in the investment business. As I watched the actual events unfold, I realized they were far worse than I had anticipated, or possibly could have anticipated given my propensity to see too many glasses as half full. I never put money on the downside and made no profit thereby. I simply escaped most of the carnage.

Watching the unfolding disaster drew me back to a close following of the economic news. It was a terrible but fascinating spectacle; the economics were intellectually riveting, while the human dramas were frightening. Crisis may be an overused and devalued word, but there is no doubt that the financial markets were in crisis in the fall of 2008, and had that crisis not been effectively managed, which for the most part it was, the ramifications for the United States and the world could have been devastating. We would be in a far worse position than the admittedly deep mess we find ourselves in now. I'm grateful that when the chips were down, the politicians did some big things right.

In retrospect, I think my view of Wall Street was naïve. I remember once when a new receptionist joined our firm. She was a very bright woman, of early middle age and with a graduate degree in social work, and she confessed to me that she wasn't sure how she would fit in at an investment firm when all of her work experience had been as a social worker. I advised her to relax, and explained that it was basically the same type of work. The arch of her eyebrows reflected her disbelief, though she obviously didn't want to argue with management on her first day on the job.

My explanation was straight from efficient markets theory. I told her that when the universe of money managers do their jobs well, the societal benefit is that the financial markets become more efficient. More efficient financial markets, by definition, will lower the cost of capital to business versus less efficient markets. When the cost of capital to business falls, economic growth accelerates. A more rapidly expanding economy leads to rising employment and income levels, which in turn pulls individuals and families out of poverty. Social work, right? Or, she could simply look at the more direct impact of our business. We labored to increase the returns for our accounts, including our many foundation and endowment accounts, and when we were successful the higher funding levels allowed these institutions to more aggressively pursue their charitable objectives. Either way, it always sounded like pretty effective social work to me. That is of course why Wall Street exists. The common function of all firms involved in the debt and equity markets is to deliver the societal benefits of efficient credit and capital markets, not simply to make a few people rich. I'm not sure if she accepted it all, but I know that I did, and throughout my business career. In fact, I still do despite the tsunami of greed, short-sightedness, and stupidity that took over Wall Street.

Of course, it wasn't just Wall Street that ushered the economy into the deep recession of 2008–2009. There were many players, acting from good motives and bad, and scattered not just from Washington to Wall Street, but on Main Streets around the country. In the end, there was disillusion, disappointment, disgust, and dishonesty. The disillusion and disappointment were global, and reflected the shock wave felt when U.S. financial companies and practices, long admired as the best in the world, came up so wanting. The disgust focused on those executives, financial and otherwise, who abandoned their fiduciary obligations for personal gain. Finally, the episode was crowned with dishonesty as no one had the courage to admit any part in the fiasco—not the Wall Street executives, not the rating agencies, not the regulators, not the politicians, no one. Fortunately, the United States is blessed with some world-class reporters who sorted through the rubble and told the story well.

My own disgust with what had happened in the world of finance, and with the orgy of finger pointing that erupted in the wake of the debacle, prompted me to turn the channel for a while, ignore the financial news, and sail off the calendar.

It has been a long and wet day at the helm. I change into some equally grubby but much drier clothes and immediately feel better. The problem with sea-wet clothes is that they're full of salt crystals, which absorb and capture enough moisture that your clothes always feel clammy (or crusty, depending on how much salt you're asking them to carry). They will never fully dry until you give them a good freshwater rinse, another reason to keep your foul-weather gear on. One little miscreant of a wave and you're dripping. Come to think of it, I could use a freshwater rinse myself.

I enjoy a bowl of stew while listening to Art Tatum on piano and Benny Carter on alto saxophone playing "Under a Blanket of Blue." It's a wonderful title for blue-water listening, and a piece you can listen to all night long.

FRIENDS AND FAMILY

*To reach the port of heaven, we must sail
sometimes with the wind and sometimes against it,
but we must sail, and not drift, nor lie at anchor.*

—OLIVER WENDELL HOLMES, SR.

I woke during the night to find *Rubicon* right on course and moving well with Juribass. What a pleasant surprise! Perhaps it was a good idea naming this contrary contraption. The wind is in the high teens, the waves have dropped, and with the main and solent sails showing their full selves to the world, *Rubicon* is looking like a sailboat, or would be if she didn't still have the half dozen pieces of monofilament line trailing from the topping lift, the remains of the broken Dutchman system of last week. It is an easy job to drop the topping lift and remove the now useless lines, and I soon have them stuffed in a duffel bag. Looks count, and we look a damn sight better now. Munching my way through the day, I consume handfuls of nuts, mugs of tea, a can of tuna from the stack that never seems to get depleted, a very forlorn-looking apple, and a can of pears. I also find a jar of salsa and a bag of chips, which put a smile on my face until I realize that the bottom of the bag has split and I have left a trail of chips about the boat like Hansel and Gretel. Feeling very righteous, if a tad bloated, from all this healthy food, I do my daily rounds, inspecting *Rubicon* for any chafing lines, loose fittings, or other potential problems. When I pull up the floorboard to look in the bilge, I do a double-take. There is only the usual and nominal amount of water in the bilge, but today it's black. I immediately suspect that the engine has leaked oil, which has seeped down to the bilge and blackened the water. I wonder if this will be the problem du jour, if I will have to limp into Newport with dead batteries because the engine is on the disabled list. However, after conducting a thorough inspection of the engine compartment, all seems in order. It's a puzzle that I decide to mull over while I move on to other work.

The next task is to give the boat a thorough cleaning after the heavy weather and on-deck preoccupations of recent days. To conserve energy the power to the refrigerator has been off for many days, but it still serves as an effective cooler. It's time to give a feast to the fish of whatever foodstuffs remain and clean out the box. It does not take long to discover that a large jar of jelly has lost its cap and clumps of purple goo are everywhere, including clogging the unit's drain to the bilge. There has been no oil spill on the boat, just a grape jelly spill! I enjoy a good laugh at my earlier concerns. No problems du jour yet.

A bottle of champagne and the remaining half a jar of grape jelly are now the only items left from my purging of the frig. The champagne was given to me by Huw, a great friend and my coskipper in the double-handed leg of the Bermuda 1-2 Race. Huw brought the gift when he traveled from Scotland to Plymouth to visit for a few days, and of course he spent most of that time helping to prepare *Rubicon* for her return passage. We had planned to open the bottle when Barbara arrived. She flew to Plymouth for the week to help with the project, and to do a little joint sightseeing. We never got around to pouring the bubbly, so we decided to save it for celebratory toasts in Newport.

We live in a culture where friends, and indeed families, rotate into and out of our lives. My birth family is now gone, the extended part having passed away in the old country and the nuclear family having detonated in the new country. My family by marriage has mostly rotated away, without rancor or bitterness, but seemingly as a way of the world, though they remain supporting actors in the children's lives. A new family has rotated into my life. I hope to keep it. Apart from my children, family now lacks the permanence I always associated with the word.

Our culture often values the appearance of friendship more than the thing itself. Has a politician or entertainer ever introduced someone without calling them "my friend," often "my dear friend"? Whenever you're introduced as a dear friend, hold on to your wallet. True friendship is not as common as our vernacular suggests, particularly among adult men, but it is not the rarest of blessings either.

I've heard it said that our friends are God's way of apologizing to us for our families. If so, then God has been good to me. I have made some wonderful friends in business and in sailing, and sometimes, in stressful situations, gotten to know who they really are. There's David, whom I knew for many years before I ever saw him unsettled by life, and then only because the cable guy was late and the Red Sox were in the playoffs. Who could blame him? Bill, the professional sailor who has spent years of his life at sea but is connected to the world in ways that those without a passport will never understand. Kevin, the engineer technician who can get to the bottom of any problem on a boat and won't be happy until he does. Mary, who always reminds me of one of those "old souls" that people talk about, the ones who keep the "new souls" on track. And Hank, garrulous, warm-hearted, and unflappable. He has built a business for himself, created opportunities for countless sailors, and given me the graduate seminar in sailing, though I doubt he is even aware of that last fact.

It may not be necessary to be a font of new ideas in life, as long as the ones you do conjure up have some candlepower. Hank, a lifelong sailor and delivery skipper, came up with a good one, which he developed into a business and named Offshore Passage Opportunities, or OPO. It was a way of matching boat captains, either owners or delivery captains, with would-be crew. The crewmembers were amateur sailors looking to gain experience, and perhaps a dose of adventure, before returning to work and family. It was a win-win, as they say in the business world; the captain got enthusiastic and unpaid crew who, for the price of their transportation to and from the boat, grew as sailors and received wonderful deposits in their memory banks. For Hank, as long as everyone paid their dues, it was a profitable information business, which he migrated seamlessly to the world of e-mail and the Internet. And for me, it was my ticket to the world of blue water.

The OPO motto, labeled as a proverb on its website, states, "It is easier to make new friends who sail than it is to teach your old friends how to sail." I was slow in warming to this phrase; it felt harsh, like you're tossing old friends overboard. Of course that wasn't the case; the truth was you simply weren't taking them onboard for your next passage. If someone is going to pursue a passion, why not pursue it with those who hold it with the same intensity?

The wind seems to be resting in the single digits. The waves are also moving to repose, lying down, as sailors say. There is little excitement as *Rubicon* slowly glides through the seas, but a palpable and wonderful peace has descended over us—no undefined sounds, no sudden twists or lurches, no water over the bow, just this quiet march west. Yes, fast sailing is a joy, and in a race fast is better than slow, but there is nothing I can do to summon more wind, so acceptance is part of the program, and here, now, it is not difficult. Being in the moment is always part of the program.

A thick fog has set in. I have never before enjoyed sailing in fog; it has just been one more weight on the wrong side of the risk–return scales. Today, with nothing to bump into for hundreds of miles except another boat, and my AIS and radar systems on the job, I refuse to let the fog affect my spirits. Having put aside the worry, the beauty emerges. *Rubicon* is gliding across a stage, with the curtain constantly rising ahead of us and falling in our wake, and she's putting on a proud display. Everything is softened, and even the waves have lost their hard edges; they're all sanded down and milky gauze surrounds the stage.

It is a satisfying moment for a sailor when the passage chart can be put away and the charts for local waters retrieved from the chart locker. As my passage chart has been taped to the table below for the past two months, I decide to leave it in place but, overlaying it, I unfold the chart covering Nantucket Shoals, Narragansett Bay, and Newport. A fair wind and I will be drinking something stronger than tea before the calendar changes to July.

It is late evening and I'm sitting in the cockpit. As usual, I am wearing my harness but I have not bothered to clip the tether to any strongpoint as the night is calm. The cockpit is a pretty secure area, and I don't generally clip on unless conditions are bringing a little excitement to the party. I'm perched on the helm seat right behind the wheel when some urge prompts me to snap the shackle of my tether to the pad eye. Just as I straighten up, a wave that clearly belongs in another neighborhood breaks into the cockpit and washes out the transom. It is not a big enough fellow to knock me out of the cockpit; I'm pretty sure about that. In fact, the wave isn't much of a rogue, only confused, but the odd thing is that I don't remember hearing any untoward sound, or any of my senses reporting the wave's arrival, and I can only wonder at my decision to increase security at that moment.

TURNING THE PAGE

The finest hour, that I have seen,
Is the one that comes between
The edge of night and the break of day,
It's when the darkness rolls away.

—KATE WOLF

t is still cool and damp in the mornings, but no longer cold. I continue to wear a warm layer under my foulies, and of course my seaboots, but life on deck is comfortable. In fact, I am not simply comfortable, but content as I feast on the beauty of the morning and the serenity that prevails as we sashay along in the light air. The sky is quickly losing the full-on overcast that I have accepted as normal, and the now definable clouds that continue to punctuate the sky are retreating to allow the sun's rays to bathe *Rubicon* in a gorgeous light. This morning's sea is like a great field of grass softly swaying in the wind. While sipping my tea I decide that it's time for a dose of culture, so I dig out the one Mozart CD I have on the boat. His horn concertos sound spectacular piping through the cockpit speakers.

It occurs to me that *Rubicon* has been undercanvased for most of the race. Too much sail area and the boat is hard to control, too little and the boat is too slow, and *Rubicon* has had too little for too long. Apart from the first phase, which lasted only five days, we have carried a conservative sail plan either by choice or by necessity. The loss of the autopilot was the first catalyst, and I know I didn't push the boat for a few days while I came up to speed with Hydro. Then there was the loss of the big genoa due to the jammed furler, the temporary sidelining of the solent sail between tear and repair, the delay in resetting the full main after it came off its track, and, finally, the loss of Hydro and the requirement to hand steer or wander under the jury-rigged steering. The equipment issues are understandable, but the willingness to tolerate an undercanvased boat, which my fatigue sometimes allowed, is a black mark in my personal copybook. You can't go for so long with such a deficit in sail area and be competitive. I guess I will have to hold competitive for another time.

It's clear that I will be bringing up the rear in this race, though hopefully not last. A friend has e-mailed me saying that one of the competitors—Geoff Alcorn, an intrepid sailor who completed his qualifying sail for the OSTAR with a solo sail around Ireland—has also lost his autopilot and is hand steering to Newport. He's about a day behind me, no doubt due to a slightly slower boat. The e-mail didn't discuss particulars on the other boats, an omission that can probably be read as confirmation that everyone else is either ahead or already in Newport. I'm not sure when my OSTAR morphed from a race to a passage, but if the event requires a time stamp, it would be the moment I lost Hydro.

I am reminded of all those pithy quotes about the value of failure, but none of them call it pretty. Once, about midway through my career, I suffered a business reversal. That same month *Fortune* magazine ran a cover story with the title, "So You Fail. Now Bounce Back." I kept that magazine in my desk for years afterward, a reminder that failures are stepping-stones or roadblocks, and the choice is always ours. Well, perhaps not always, but it's best to think of them that way.

My failure was an inability to deliver superior equity performance when we started the new firm. We had hoped to develop an equity side of the business, but for that we needed strong numbers for the first two years. I had brought a fairly strong performance record with me from my years at Brown Brothers Harriman, but when a portfolio manager moves from a large firm, there is always the "portability of performance question." Potential clients wonder how much of the performance record should be attributed to the individual, and how much to the previous firm. It's a fair question, and never easy to answer fully. Institutional mandates and constraints often serve to improve the numbers, but they can also act to limit performance. Most institutional investment policy has a fair degree of flexibility within the guidelines, which further complicates the question. At the end of the day, it comes down to convincing clients that your product will work for them, just as in any other business. After two years of effort, my new track record was "market," meaning that it was in line with the market index, the good old S&P 500 large-cap stock index. Market performance may have been better than that of most active managers in those years, and quite good when looked at from this light or that—and blah, blah, blah—but not enough to get new accounts pouring in the door. As Winston Churchill once observed, "Sometimes it's not enough to do your best, you have to do what is required." But there are times when you can only do your best.

I was close to resigning after my failure to build a stock side to our new investment firm, but the bond side was doing well and we were just getting our footing. I had no illusions that my presence was crucial to the firm's success, yet having joined the firm on day one I felt duty bound, and of course financially motivated, to stay aboard until we had safely navigated to the waters of profitability. I became a bond man. Year four was our breakeven year, which was just as well, as the capital was dwindling. It was also the year Gail died, and the year I decided to stay for the duration. Among the less important developments that she never got to see was the business success of the firm.

With failure, as with grief, it is important to arrive at acceptance, and that must follow honesty. We can flavor it as we like, as with Edison who famously said, "I have not failed. I've just found 10,000 ways that don't work." This is all fine and well, but there are points in time where examinations must be made. Sometimes the data can suggest very different stories depending on the exact starting and ending points. Think of Lehman Brothers. Economists refer to this as the end-point problem. So be it. We have to look.

I have certainly failed in one of my goals for this race. I have simply not sailed a fast boat quickly enough to be competitive. Part of it was "racing luck," but in keeping with today's theme of honesty, I know that a podium finish was never very realistic. I know this from reading the bios of the other competitors. Fortunately, I also know that if we limit our goals to the realistic ones we will be the poorer for it. I can live with my standing in the race, and no doubt I'll be comfortable with it by the time I bring *Rubicon* safely into Newport harbor.

The wake streaming behind *Rubicon* is straight, and far different from those we carved as the gales of a North Atlantic spring swept over us, wakes that were snatched away by the sea before any linearity could be noted. These wakes bubble, froth, and slowly fade, taking the hours with them.

Weeks ago I made the very conscious decision to avoid thoughts of arrival, of how many days to go, or even how many days had elapsed. Each day was a page and I would stay focused on that page till the darkness gave way to the next page. Some would be better, some worse, some colder, warmer, wetter, drier, quieting, or disquieting. I would travel each one. This approach always seems so much easier at sea than on land, which is no small part of the appeal of going to sea. Here, I am not just in the moment, I am in the life.

Dinner is a disappointment as a new problem emerges: the propane safety switch is cutting off the gas after about 30 seconds of operation. A quick inspection doesn't show any obvious cause of the problem, and I suspect that the switch has broken or perhaps the solenoid at the tank has failed. In any event, the oven and stove are both now out of commission, so there is no way to heat dinner or even boil water. With the necessity of spending all available energies steering the boat, there will be no time to investigate this latest tribulation. I'm grateful it didn't happen at the start of the race; a month of cold food would have taken its toll on my morale. As it is, I will be home soon and the weather is mild. It's just another inconvenience.

The day has evaporated in a river of remembrance, most of it spent working on my self-steering system, rigging "permanent" loops at each spoke of the wheel, putting together various lines and hooks and bungees, and tweaking it for current conditions before every break from hand steering. The wind is back, the clouds are back, and we are on a fine jog, sailing on starboard tack in cool and foggy conditions. I make a last note in the log and the page turns once again.

NAVIGATION

Time is the longest distance between two places.

—TENNESSEE WILLIAMS

Today is as clear and defined as yesterday was opaque and shrouded, and our progress is a parade march powered by a very decent breeze out of the south-southwest.

Another day passes at the wheel, steering, singing, and thinking. Hand steering can be hard and exhausting work in heavy weather, an effort requiring all my concentration, but today it is easy. I can hop up on the helm seat behind the wheel and enjoy the ride while working my way through the nth repetition of my song repertoire. I've been asked many times if I ever get bored at sea, and I have always emphatically, and truthfully, denied any boredom, but hand steering for most of your waking hours day after day, unable to leave the wheel without heaving-to or watching the boat wander off course, brings a tedium that I have never before experienced at sea.

I have just reviewed *Rubicon*'s to-do list. My guess is that it will take at least two weeks of concentrated work to get *Rubicon* back in shape to go cruising after the race. Of course, there will be no need to rush, as there will be no cruising for a while. I need to attend to home responsibilities. There may be more on that to-do list than on *Rubicon*'s.

The light of the day is starting to fade, though the ship's clock shows midnight and suggests that darkness should have descended hours ago. I know that I should really have adjusted the clock for every 15 minutes of longitude traveled west, but I have been using GPS navigation, not celestial, and it has been more convenient to ignore the time specified by the orbit of the earth and simply mark time according to GMT (Greenwich Mean Time). It is also a requirement of the race that all skippers send a daily e-mail between 1200 and 1400 GMT indicating their position, and leaving the ship's clock on GMT has been a good reminder.

Another few years and only historians will use the GMT reference. UTC (Coordinated Universal Time) has now displaced GMT as the more politically correct term for a global time reference, and International Meridian has replaced Prime Meridian as the accepted term for that line of longitude, with the designation 0° 00' (zero degrees and zero minutes).

You cannot navigate without knowing what time it is—precisely what time it is. To know the place you're at, you must know the time you're in. Sailors have known this for centuries. It is now possible to delegate the time-keeping function, and today we assign it to our GPS units, or rather to the satellites that send this information to the little GPS antennas on our boats. No winding required, but I still like to have the clock onboard. There are two on *Rubicon*, the small clock at the nav station, which is set to GMT, and the larger ship's clock by the companionway, which should be set to local time but is still set to GMT.

To understand longitude, you only need to imagine placing a large hoop around the planet with the hoop passing over the North and South Poles. This is a meridian of longitude, or two actually as each half of the circle—each of the arcs from pole to pole—is considered a meridian, or line, of longitude. If we rotate this hoop around the earth while keeping it positioned over the two poles, the arcs of the hoop will have covered every possible spot on the planet, and every possible meridian of longitude from 0° 00' to 180° 00' east, or west, and back to 0° 00'. Every meridian of longitude can be described with a number and an east or west designation, such as our current longitude of 64° 35' W. The question is west or east of what, and the answer has nothing to do with the physical sciences.

It was history and politics that placed the Prime Meridian through Greenwich, England.

Longitude would be a meaningless concept if there were no reference line from which to begin counting. The prime designation could have been linked to any meridian of longitude, and indeed earlier attempts to set up the grid had cartographers placing the start line through Rome, Jerusalem, and various points in between, but we can assume that it has found its final resting place. The primacy given the line passing through Greenwich may be an accident of history, but it is also an accident of history that any one of us is here at all. I don't believe every such accident needs to be devalued or debunked, so I have taped the label GMT below the small clock at the nav station.

Arcs of latitude are known as parallels because they are a series of circles, equally spaced from, and parallel to, the equator. Meridians of longitude are all equal in distance, or would be if the earth were a perfect sphere, but parallels of latitude have different lengths, with the equator being the greatest of the great circles. The parallels of latitude become shorter as they approach the poles, and we can even imagine a tiny circle of latitude less than an inch long surrounding the point that is the pole. There are 180 degrees of latitude between the North Pole at 90° 00' N and its southern counterpart at 90° 00' S. The equator (00° 00') could have been called the Prime Parallel, as that is the starting line for all the parallels, but we simply call it the equator. Where to place the equator was not an accident of history. It was obvious once we understood the physical orientation of our world.

At any moment in time we are at the intersection of a line of latitude and a line of longitude. If we know those coordinates, our lat–lon as sailors say, we know our exact location. If we know our latitude we know exactly how far we are, either north or south, from the equator, and if we know our longitude, we know our exact distance east or west of the Prime Meridian.

Finding latitude has always been a much more straightforward affair than determining longitude because astronomers and navigators have known that the height of the sun at noon varies depending on the distance from the equator, being low in the sky at the poles and very high at the equator. Measurements of the sun's height above the horizon were taken at local noon, which is when the sun would be at its highest point relative to that location. If the sun wasn't at its highest point, it wasn't local noon. The clock was not critical.

Finding longitude was a tougher nut to crack. As Dava Sobel observed in her jewel of a book, *Longitude*, finding latitude was "child's play" while longitude was "an adult dilemma—one that stumped the wisest minds of the world for the better part of human history." To find longitude, seafarers needed an instrument capable of measuring the angle of a celestial body above the horizon—usually the sun, sometimes the moon, and occasionally the stars—and they needed to know the precise time, not only locally, but also back at the Prime Meridian. As the earth's rotation causes the sun to move 15 degrees of longitude in every hour, the time differential was a key to the puzzle, and that required a highly accurate timepiece.

Modern sextants have been around since the middle 1700s and, given enough practice and a break in the clouds, these instruments can capture the angular clues to the puzzle. However, these angles of altitude were quite useless unless you knew the exact time of the measurement because, of course, the angle was constantly changing. Developing an accurate timepiece—particularly one that could withstand the rigors of a sea life with its constant turbulence and daily changes in heat and humidity—was a long process, but success may be dated from the 1760s when the masterpieces that were the clocks of John Harrison started going to sea. Harrison was the winner of the longitude prize established by the British Parliament as an incentive for someone to solve the riddle of finding longitude at sea. Despite years of delay, his beautiful, accurate, and rugged chronometers secured the prize, and the honor and wealth that accompanied it. With accurate chronometers, the ability to measure angles, and the knowledge of where a particular celestial body was supposed to be at a particular time—information increasingly available in the eighteenth century—many sailors were spared a watery grave, and British sea power took another leap forward.

The larger ship's clock is on the bulkhead by the companionway and now, with *Rubicon* less than 350 miles to the finish, it is past time to synchronize the ship's clock with the New World. It is time to move to time zone 5, which covers Newport and the rest of the eastern seaboard. Each of the world's time zones, as opposed to time adjustments made for political or economic reasons such as daylight saving time, covers 15 degrees of longitude, and this relates to that 15-degree-arc-per-hour pace of the sun. Twenty-four times fifteen is 360 degrees, and that is the circle that the ancients thought the sun traveled as it circled the earth, and was the Ptolemaic view. However, Copernicus believed, and Galileo proved, that the sun's movement was simply a perception caused by the earth's west-to-east rotation on its axis, and that the rotating earth was actually circling the sun. The beauty of it is that the angles are what the angles are, and it doesn't matter whether you agree with Ptolemy or Galileo; if you have a nautical almanac, an accurate watch, and a sextant, you can find longitude.

Putting my finger to the slender black arm of the clock, I bring *Rubicon* to her proper time, and a feeling of accomplishment washes over me, a belief that home draws near.

With so much food on the boat, as well as a case of MREs, there should be something that can be prepared without a stove. While pondering the possible culinary choices for dinner, I suddenly realize that duct tape, the one item no sailor ever goes to sea without, could once again come to the rescue. All I needed to do was shift my engine-charging schedule to late afternoon or early evening, depending on how hungry I was. I immediately put the plan into effect. After cutting a longish strip of duct tape, I secured one of the MRE's foil dinner pouches to the top of the engine manifold and turned on the engine. Some 45 minutes later I pulled the duct tape off the hot engine, cut open the pouch, and squeezed a nice hot dinner onto my plate.

I'm sitting in the cockpit of *Rubicon*, looking out over a darkening sea as the sun slides behind a cloudbank on her way over the horizon. It's a delicious scene, which is more than I can say for the plate of chili and beans that I'm spooning. Chili is one of my specialties, but this is the U.S. government's recipe, not mine. This chili has smothered and defeated a slab of Wasa crispbread, which before meeting the chili had the consistency of a roofing tile. Despite its sludgy appearance and overspiced taste, I congratulate myself on laying in a stock of these provisions, and on my manifold cooking. The food is hearty and warming, and it's comforting that I now have a way to enjoy some hot dinners on these last days of the passage. Unfortunately, I can see no way to boil water, so tca and coffee are still off the menu.

A SHEARWATER'S VISIT

Tourists know where they've been.
Travelers don't know where they're going.
—PAUL THEROUX

We have company this morning, a graceful brown bird that has turned gliding into an art form. It seems to require very little wing movement to gain back some altitude, and then it's off on another long swoop over and behind the waves. I've been trying to identify it from my *Field Guide to North Atlantic Wildlife* and I'm pretty sure it's a shearwater, specifically a Cory shearwater. I would need stronger glasses and a nonrocking boat to tell the difference between some of the birds pictured in the book, but it does seem to match the description, and the solo appearance fits the pattern. Many other shearwaters arrive in company. According to the guidebook, the shearwaters got their name because their wingtips appear to slice the side of the waves as they pursue their low-altitude quest for food. Watching this one come in low and fast, they do appear to be aptly named. It is captivating to watch these long arcs filled with grace and fluidity, but I don't see any fish catching going on. Perhaps this one had breakfast before I got on deck and is just checking out *Rubicon*.

We have the wind from behind today and *Rubicon* is moving well, but the Juribass system just can't handle the deep downwind sailing, so if I need to accomplish any task other than steering I simply heave-to. Rest at the expense of progress is no virtue, so I keep the breaks short.

As I look about *Rubicon*, I think of how far she's come from the tuned machine that raced down the English Channel five weeks ago. The repair list may be long, but to my eye she's still one beautiful yacht. I use the word "yacht" sparingly these days. The word comes from the Dutch word "Jacht," meaning "hunt." In the age of sail the Dutch and other navies used fast, small, and lightly armed sailboats to pursue pirates and smugglers when they tried to hide in shallow waters. It's been a long time since the navies of the world included yachts in their fleets. Yachts are all recreational now, and come in every shape and size. Some definitions state that a yacht may be as short as 26 feet, though there is no upper limit in size. There are motoryachts and sailing yachts, superyachts and megayachts and, of course, luxury yachts, which sounds redundant but isn't. Most megayachts are the floating condominiums found in the destination harbors of the world. I would no doubt enjoy hanging my hat in one for a spell, sitting at the onboard bar surveying the harbor with a drink in my hand, but I cannot think of these vessels as yachts. The noun has morphed over the years. Words can change their meanings over time, or one meaning can eclipse all the others and it can become difficult to use them in certain contexts. That's the nature of language; words rise and fall and change, and that's fine, though I miss the word "yacht." It's still with us of course, perhaps more than ever, but I find it an awkward word unless I'm using it as a modifier, as in "yacht race" or "yacht club." "Yacht" was a perfectly fine word, and one with a strong and pleasing sound, perfect for conveying the beauty of a sailing craft. And beautiful they are. I agree with Arthur Beiser, who wrote in his book *The Proper Yacht*, "I start from the premise that no object created by man is as satisfying to his body and soul as a proper sailing yacht." The noun was corrupted in our era of excess, and the definition that springs to most minds is that of a rich person's toy, or so it seems. I don't know that it's politically incorrect to use the word "yacht," but I find it hard to say the word without feeling that I'm putting on airs. I now prefer "sloop," or "sailboat," or simply "*Rubicon*."

■ ▪ ■

The winds went fluky around midday, just as we passed 66° W, and it is a hard afternoon's work to keep us on track. It's overcast and raining lightly and the soft and shifty winds make for wide jibing angles, so the directional choices are limited. I'll take southeast and take my chances with any remnants of the Gulf Stream.

The ache fades from my arms while I take a break and enjoy the rain. There's not much wind anyway. A bottle of "nutritionally enhanced" water sits on the table, water flavored by a small packet of energy drink mix, one of the little goodies they include in the MRE packs along with the entree, a cookie, jelly, etc., but no more of the small ten-packs of cigarettes that used to come in the C-rations. Different brands came in each box and we used to trade them in the field, a pack of Salem for a pack of Camels or Marlboros. Of course, Marlboros were in the highest demand. I think the Marlboro Man appealed to the mind-sets of the young marines. I know he did to mine.

I love the sound of the rain hitting the boat, not the sound of waves crashing over the bow, or the assault of a driving rain, but the patter of a steady soaker while I'm snug and dry in the warm embrace of my wood-paneled home. I close my eyes and I'm a Boy Scout again, sitting in a tent and listening to the rain. There's been some inflation in my definition of snug since then, but this certainly qualifies.

The silky voice of Norah Jones saturates the cabin as the rain continues to fall. I have listened to her lyrics many times, but never have they felt so apt. You can almost feel her breath as she reveals her vision of a future shared only with the listener, following every delightful detail of what life could be with the seductive refrain, "Come Away with Me." It's not really a question, and hardly a command, simply a suggestion that would be difficult for any sane man to resist. Yet, just as the last notes from the piano are fading, the very welcome picture in my mind of the beautiful Norah Jones is replaced by the grizzled countenance of Bernard Moitessier, RIP, the spiritual father of all solo sailors. A similar song must have played in Moitessier's mind when he abandoned the first solo around-the-world yacht race. He did this in the latter stage of the

race when he was already in the South Atlantic, pointed toward the
finish in English waters and with the full knowledge that he would
be the likely winner. He had a good lead and preparations for his
arrival had begun, a landfall where honor and glory awaited, not to
mention the prize money of five thousand pounds, a small fortune
for an itinerant sailor. Instead, he chose to head east, passing the
Cape of Good Hope and crossing the Indian Ocean, both for the
second time since leaving Falmouth harbor, and finally arriving in
the Pacific, where he found the islands he loved. He sent a message
via a passing ship, saying, "I am continuing nonstop because I am
happy at sea and perhaps to save my soul." This always struck me
as a good thing because it allowed an Englishman, Robin Knox-
Johnston, later knighted by the queen, to win the race. It was also an
admirable thing. Moitessier was a romantic who was not at home in
the modern world of 1968. He went where he needed to go.

I can't go away with *Rubicon* though. My jaunt to Plymouth
and back will no doubt define the outer limit of my sailing radius,
no Marquesas or Tahiti, no transit of the Panama Canal. I have no
such temptations, or none that I will allow to show. I am an Atlantic
sailor and I'm fine with that. I cannot run away to the sea, and as
for my soul, it may be nourished at sea, but if it is to be saved it will
be on land.

The wind has shifted to the northwest and we're hard on the
wind again, but for a while life is much easier. With a little help
from Juribass, *Rubicon* can hold a proper course and I seize the
opportunity for a nap. Lying down is a sensual experience. The mat
no longer feels hard against my back, or anything less than totally
inviting, and I'm soon captured by sleep. An hour later I wake to
find the sails aback. So it goes. It is strange that it takes some doing
to get *Rubicon* moving again. Perhaps we're both tired.

BEST SEAT IN
THE HOUSE

May you live every day of your life.
—JONATHAN SWIFT

t was noisy and beautiful last night. Noisy because we were becalmed, and the boat's quivering as the low waves rolled by kept
the sails slapping, but beautiful with a radiant moon shining on a
gentle ocean, all blacks and silvers creating a vast sequined tapestry. I
stood in the cockpit enjoying the scene until fatigue trumped both
beauty and noise and I banked a few hours of sleep. Despite the
clouds of the days, recent nights have been the most spectacular of
the passage; you just drink them in.

The radio has come to life with frequent chatter, fishing boats
mostly. The VHF (very high frequency) radio has a much shorter
range than the single-sideband radio, where the signal bounces
off the ionosphere and can transmit great distances. I have heard
VHF transmitters out to a hundred miles from a tall and powerful
transmitter, such as the one in Bermuda, but the range is generally
less than fifteen miles, so the radio has been quiet for most of the
trip. More land birds are coming out to greet *Rubicon*; signs of life
abound.

I notice that despite having the three reefs in the main to keep
it secured, the top batten on the mainsail has broken; no doubt a
result of the incessant shaking the sail has received. Damn! The
battens, like the interior scaffolding in a hooped skirt, are there
to help the material keep a certain shape. The broken batten will

mean that the top part of the sail will not hold its shape as well as it should, but this is not of great import. The top batten, where the sail is narrowest, has a lighter workload than the lower ones, but as I have brought no spare battens, it will just be one more aggravation to live with till Newport.

A light wind, perhaps 5 to 8 knots, returns around midmorning and gives us a knot or two of boat speed. I finish the page I'm reading, shake out the reefs, and we are moving again, slowly but in the right direction. I am paroled from the wheel for much of the day as the Juribass system is holding a pretty decent course, so the time is spent studying the weather maps, cleaning the boat, and finishing John Grisham's *The King of Torts*, a fun read about lawyers waging big class-action suits.

It looked to be clearing earlier when there was no wind, but now the light wind has delivered a heavy fog, not what I would have expected. Sometimes the breeze takes the fog away and sometimes it brings it in. I have grown to enjoy sailing in fog, but only away from shore with little to hit or be hit by—it suggests a private and mysterious realm. We are sliding stealthily across the seascape. There is timelessness to the experience, and serenity.

The weather maps don't suggest much wind so I guess my arrival will be when it will be, but it won't be tomorrow. I had hoped to be in Newport before June expired, and with so few miles to the finish, a smile from the wind gods could have made it so. But it is not to be, and I have to accept that my arrival date will now have a July handle on it. I have to wonder if I will make it to Newport by the deadline—after 11:59 p.m. on July 5 you are no longer considered an official finisher. Is it less of an achievement if you miss this designation? It is not a question I want to consider. I can't give up! I hear myself say, "Ruby, you and I will sail into Newport, and we will do it before the deadline. And when we sail in, we will arrive looking sharp."

Just as my mind turns to food, the AIS alarm sounds and I look at the small screen to see what ship will be visiting the neighborhood today. I find that it is not just any ship. It is the *Queen Mary*, actually the *Queen Mary 2*, as the original is now a floating hotel in California. I've seen the *Queen Mary 2* at close range in

New York Harbor and she looks like the majestic liners of old, very much like the original except that she has one stack instead of three. I look again at the screen and see that she is steaming to New York at 23 knots and will pass about 2 miles off. At that speed I could be in Newport to catch a nightcap. I grab the binoculars to watch her pass, but the lingering fog obscures her fine lines.

The sun, wherever it is, is now lighting some other part of our planet; it has stolen the wind and, at least for the moment, the serenity I have enjoyed this day. *Rubicon* is becalmed again, but I am not, and I send the following e-mail to a friend and supporter:

> *To say that I'm absolutely and totally fed up would be an understatement. I am sitting here in the proverbial millpond going nowhere. In fact, I have three reefs in the main to stop it banging around so much as the boat rocks back and forth. The noise was starting to drive me crazy (not a long trip right now) and I was afraid something would break. There is no wind! I'm still 208 miles from the finish and there is a part of me that says this is crazy. I've run a good race, if not a competitive one, despite numerous setbacks and perhaps I should just put the engine in gear (I could do that with a pair of Vise-Grips in the engine compartment) and bring her on in. However, I can't do that. I've had a lot of supporters in this project and I feel that I would be letting them down. Also, I don't want to send a message to Steven and Amy that quitting is OK to do if the road gets hard. There is also the fact that this is an international competition and I'm the only American in the race. And last but definitely not least, I want to know that I sailed across the Atlantic with no asterisk to the achievement. So, when all is said and done, I'm here for the duration. I don't know when I will arrive, perhaps Thursday, but I will sail in.*

I hit the send button, sit back, and then the lightbulb goes on. I need to get a grip! Of course I'm ready to get in, ready to sip a beer, absorb the smiles of loved ones, park myself under a shower, and all the rest, but I'm in the best seat in the house watching the ever-changing theater of the sea. I'm in no danger. I still have ample stocks of food, water, and books. I need to get over myself. How did I let that beautiful serenity of this morning slip away? I put a CD in the stereo, Chopin's Concerto no. 2, and go on deck. My frustration drifts off into the fog as I absorb the pageantry of another night at sea.

As Gilda Radner used to say, "It's always something." I've had a lot of somethings on this trip, but none of them really amount to much. They are inconveniences, hardly losses. Real losses are irredeemable. You move on, but they are always a part of you, holes in your humanity that you plug with memories.

One afternoon, about two months after Gail died, I was returning to my office from a meeting in the city and bumped into an old Wall Street acquaintance, a technology analyst who was by then running his own tech fund. We chatted for a few minutes. He had heard of my loss, and expressed his condolences by saying, "I know what you're going through, I remember how tough it was when I went through my divorce. It's very hard, but the worst part is behind you now." I could feel my blood pressure rising as I thought, *What do you mean you know how I feel?* There's no comparison between the sudden death of a spouse and a divorce. And what's this crap about the worst part being behind me? I was dizzy with the job of just carrying on in those early months. Never before or since have I felt such a strong desire to launch my fist into the person on the other side of a conversation. Fortunately, that certain reserve that keeps us all out of jail, and some dim awareness that his thoughts were launched with kind intent kept my hands at my side. We chatted aimlessly for a few more minutes before going our separate ways.

The memory of that encounter has stayed with me over the years, but my reading of it has changed. I have come to realize, with only slight reluctance, that he was right. Worse than that, he was right on both counts. Who was I to think that I could measure another's depth of pain? And to what purpose anyway? Pain is pain, and grief and loss visit us all. Perhaps everyone's pain is unique, though I'm more than a little skeptical about that, but it no longer strikes me as important. We all experience the knockout blows sooner or later, so it is universal. In fact, after death and taxes, loss has to be one of the building blocks of the human condition. Loss in all its forms, sudden and vicious, or slow and withering, it has either paid us a visit or it's on the way. Getting up after a knockout blow, finding new purpose or reaffirming old goals, and putting one foot in front of another is a call to arms. We must respond or retreat into cowardice.

I thought his comments were clueless at the time, but I was really the clueless one; clueless and angry and waiting for someone to strike a match. OK, perhaps his condolences fell short of the tact suggested by the occasion, but he was a tech guy after all; he had made the effort to say something, and he was honest and he was right. Change and loss are the universal constants that we must all accept. Only then can we seek new purpose, and find our crutch to go on. My duties were clear, but sailing has been my crutch. I'm grateful that I found it.

As midnight approaches, the sky clears and a light breeze arrives, one with just enough force to give purpose to our movement. The moon is down, and the heavens display their constellations, stars in their multitudes glittering like splinters of polished crystal. I turn the navigation lights off for a time, cutting out these feeble artificial lights while I stand breathless in the face of nature's theater. The lingering embarrassment from my earlier e-mail is gone and peace returns; holding this sense of peace when I return to civilization will be the challenge.

COMING TO AMERICA

Immigration is the sincerest form of flattery.

—JACK PARR

The AIS alarm is wailing, more of a chime than a wail actually, but I now realize that it has been background noise for too long. I'm a light sleeper at sea, but I must have slipped into some deep REM zone. I'm awake now! Throwing off the blanket, I take the two steps to the nav table to find the AIS screen showing a ship just over 2 miles away. The reference line reads, "No CPA," meaning that the CPA (closest point of approach) is now history. She passed close by while I was sleeping. A look at the ship's course, and *Rubicon*'s, suggests that we crossed less than a mile from each other. A mile at sea is nothing; the ship was on my doorstep, or vice versa. I step into the cockpit and see what I briefly perceive as two small boats, but then I realize that I'm looking at the two ends of one very large ship. There is also a fishing boat visible way off to port. It's getting crowded in the neighborhood. I give them a wave through the blackness and once again remind myself to be extra vigilant now that we're back in coastal waters.

Breakfast without hot tea or coffee is dreary, so I add an extra measure of marmalade to my plank of Wasa and eat it slowly as I enjoy the wind building to a light but very sailable 10 to 12 knots, nice peaceful sailing. I have become very skeptical of the idea that any given wind is not a sailable wind; sometimes it's not, but almost always it is. In life we can just motor along and wait for that perfect wind, not too strong, not too soft, and from just the right direction. Then we can unfurl our sails, put an eye to the compass, and show the world what we are here for. We can also sit at home waiting for a supermodel to come knocking on the door complaining of loneliness. It's best to press on, and assume that any wind is sailable until proven otherwise.

It is another day of heavy fog over Georges Bank, but still a fine day under sail before the wind starts to fade, and now both the wind and the afternoon have slipped away. I glance at the Windex at the top of the mast and it immediately does a 360° spin, the breeze too faint to even stabilize the needle. No sooner had I written my notes about most winds being sailable when my sailable wind deserted me. Whether the glass is half full or half empty may be a philosophical question, but you do need the glass.

I am using the time away from the wheel to review the navigation for the final stretch and generally get the boat sorted out. One very satisfying job is the removal of the plastic and duct tape wrapping from the windlass (the winch that controls the anchor chain). This important piece of gear is right at the bow of the boat and has deflected a river of salt water since leaving Newport last April. It was good to keep it well covered and protected, but now it should be available. We will be at anchoring depths shortly, and good seamanship requires that you be able to drop the anchor quickly in coastal waters. A pouch of beef stew is strapped to the engine manifold, and I tick off a few more items from the list while waiting for the batteries to charge and dinner to heat.

I cannot recall how many times I have crossed this ocean, almost always at great altitude, but the only transits that remain vivid are my first passage, and of course the current slingshot to England and back. My first crossing was on the good ship *Fairsea* in 1957. We took the night train from London to Scotland, then boarded at Glasgow for the passage across the North Atlantic and down the St. Lawrence Seaway to Quebec. We were nine days at sea, high adventure for a six-year-old.

It can fairly be said that we were accidental immigrants to America, as it had never been a part of the plan. The choices, I was later told, were Australia and Canada, and my parents had chosen Canada. I once asked my father why we had not immigrated directly to the United States, and he told me that Canada was a part of the British Commonwealth. He said that the sun may have set on the British Empire, but it never sets on the Commonwealth. Whatever the practical or patriotic pull of the Commonwealth, that reality paled against the offer of a real job, which came some months after our arrival in Canada and required the family to relocate to the United States. You could say we took the great circle route to America, as we crossed the border at Buffalo, and traveling by train we arrived in White Plains, New York, on Thanksgiving Day, totally puzzled why everything was closed.

My later study of economics fleshed out the story that the 1956–57 recession in the United States had been tough on Canada, which was then primarily a resource-driven economy, and when the great economic engine of the United States slowed, Canada ground to a halt. This was not a time when you researched job opportunities on the Internet and e-mailed your resume to prospective employers. In those days you simply walked off the ship with your bags and your family and hunted down a job. My father was an engineer, and I think he liked the job he landed just across the state border in Connecticut; despite takeovers, mergers, and corporate reorganizations, he never left it.

I wonder what they would think now. My father and I were both passionate armchair sailors. Shortly after Dad's death, my sister suggested I take his sailing books, as I was the only boating enthusiast in the family. I was shocked to discover that my own embarrassingly large sailing library had doubled. He never owned a boat, and to my knowledge never set foot on a sailboat. By the time I made the armchair-to-blue-water transition, Dad was too infirm to leave the house.

Mom was cut from a different cloth. When I purchased my first boat I invited her to visit it. She was already into her eighties, and dealing with her own infirmities, so it was more of a courtesy invitation, but she gave it a proper reply. "Peter," she said, and as always in her clipped English accent it sounded like "Pita." "Pita, I made a vow when we arrived in Canada that I would never set foot on a boat again." She had not felt my sense of adventure on our sea voyage to North America, but of course I had not been responsible for four children, one still in diapers. When I did my first solo passage, from Bermuda to New Jersey, Mom was heard to say, "It's surprising; he was always such a sensible boy."

Mom was born in 1917 in the town of Brentwood, now a part of greater London. Her father was a railway man who died young and left her mother to bring up their four children. Mom became a nurse through an apprenticeship and study program at a London hospital, and in a remarkable piece of timing she graduated the month that the United Kingdom—or more formally, the United Kingdom of Great Britain and Northern Ireland—entered the Second World War. Soldiers from Northern Ireland fought alongside English, Welsh, and Scottish troops for just shy of six years, and there was no shortage of demand for nurses.

Being well schooled in the stiff-upper-lip approach to life, and following that familiar track where émigrés become ever more like their image of the old country, I think Mom became more British than the British. One afternoon Barbara and I were going to visit Mom, who was quite frail by then but still reading the *New York Times* every day. Barbara told me on the drive up that she wanted to draw Mom out on her experiences in London during the Blitz. I suspected that my mother harbored a few stories, but thought it unlikely that we would hear them. Nevertheless, I wished Barbara well. We enjoyed a pleasant lunch and were sipping our tea when Barbara launched her gambit. "So tell me Margaret, it must have been extraordinary being a nurse in London during the war." My mother got a far-off look in her eyes, stared into a corner of the room, and said, "Most inconvenient." We didn't get much more, only the revelation that getting around the rubble-strewn streets on a bicycle could be "awkward." On the drive back, Barbara was incredulous. "That's it? What about the bombings, the fires, the human drama of it? 'Most inconvenient,' that's it?" I told Barbara that Mom obviously liked her or she wouldn't have opened up. I couldn't resist, but I was disappointed also. I had no doubt that Mom held some powerful stories from the war years, but they would no doubt die with her.

I don't believe they're looking down on me now, but I do think of them out here and wonder what they would think of their boy, whose love for the sea began while they were dreaming of life in the New World.

My parents brought me to the states in an immigrant ship. I brought my infant children in a jet plane. We were all involuntary immigrants, technically first generation, having been born in the old country (more accurately second generation, in reality, living in the foggy patch in between). I used to kid Gail that she was the only native-born citizen in the family.

Sometimes I wonder how my life would have played out if I'd grown up in England, if my parents had not brought me to America. Sometimes I wonder how the lives of my children would have played out if they had grown up in Chile, if Gail and I had not brought them to America. Were my siblings and I better off with a chance to become Americans? My parents differed on the question after they got here. Was I better off? Are my children better off as Americans? I hope so. They are hypothetical questions, the answers impossible to know, but if you are an involuntary immigrant, or you have made your children involuntary immigrants, it's nice to feel comfortable with these questions. Affections and allegiances are not always bound to the nationality of your passport.

I've always identified with immigrants and thought of myself as an immigrant, this despite the fact that I had no direct role in the decision. It's odd that while I often think of myself as an immigrant, I rarely think of my nationality. When I do, I mostly consider myself an American. But having grown up in my parents' house, I will always feel part English. In fact, growing up in that house, it's surprising that I didn't return and run for Parliament. If growing up in a transplanted English family felt so different, I don't know if I can imagine what it would feel like to arrive in the States without any fluency in English. Besides being a child and knowing the language, my experience was easier because I didn't stand out. I guess I didn't look like an immigrant to many people, and as the years went by and my English accent faded, I didn't sound like one either.

It may be inconsistent, but I never think of my children as immigrants. They arrived in diapers and have spent their lives in the

United States. I think of them as having been born in the United States, though they were given life in Santiago. However, my children each have their own sense of connection to that beautiful South American country flanked by the grandeur of the Andes and the vast expanse of the Pacific.

A light breeze is flirting with us as we nudge over the cusp between drifting and sailing. It's a lovely repeat of last night with a clearing sky and visiting stars, and I listen to Horowitz play a Tchaikovsky piano concerto as I adjust the control lines on the wheel. The sails catch the air as if taking a deep breath, and we're on the move again.

CHOPIN'S VARIATIONS

You can never go home again, but the truth is
you can never leave home, so it's all right.

—MAYA ANGELOU

The day is warm and clear, a fine day to arrive in Newport, though that's not likely to happen in the 10 knots or so of breeze currently driving us. *Rubicon* is sliding through the low waves and looking very presentable; hidden are the bags of garbage stuffed in the lazarette. The only cloud is the one in my mind wondering how long this period of calms and very light winds will last, and suggesting that just perhaps we won't make it past Castle Hill Lighthouse by the cutoff time, but once more I shove that thought overboard.

I didn't bring much classical music with me, except Mozart of course, but all afternoon I've been listening to Chopin's Piano Concerto no. 2. It was first played as a solo piece by Frederic himself. We don't have a recording of that, but it must have been something. I once heard it played by a full orchestra. It was marvelous. Probably not better or worse, just what it was. I think that what we do for ourselves versus what we do in community, and what we expect others to do for themselves versus acting in community, are questions worth grappling with—in sailing, in relationships, in government, and sometimes in parenting.

Finally, I can see the end of the passage. This OSTAR has been a strain at times, and some will no doubt refer to my voyage as a long passage, but it will be counted in days and weeks; not a long passage at all really. Becoming a sailor has been a long passage, one that has paralleled, and perhaps at a few rare moments eclipsed, the passage of single parenting. Both have brought their rewards and, at times, a little heavy weather.

A friend once told me that single parenting had brought out my feminine side. I took it as a compliment, so perhaps there has been a soupçon of personal growth. I know that I was fortunate in many ways, starting with the fact that I entered the arena at forty-five, when I owned my own home and had a decent job. I wasn't prepared, but I had structure and, of course, I had the nannies. Generals may strategize to a victory, but it's the sergeants who bring it home. I needed a sergeant; more specifically, I needed a nanny to get the job done. I started by turning away the most qualified person, my mother-in-law, who would no doubt have defined excellence in the job. It was almost an issue between us, but I feared that her role as grandmother would be compromised, and the children needed her in that role. Fortunately, Claire understood.

My first approach was to work through an employment agency that could do the reference and background checks. I thought a mature, middle-aged woman would be perfect, and no doubt the right one would have been, but we didn't find the right one. I fired the first two nannies that I'd employed through the agency, and decided to take a more independent approach after that.

Firing people is a foul job, but I did have to fire A~ after Amy told me that she was scared to be in the car with her. I gave A~ a short road test and I was scared too. She had a clean driving record, at least according to the referral agency, but apparently that proved little. I had no choice. Unfortunately, her replacement also had to go. C~ would have her coat on and be standing by the door when I got home from work, hardly the sign of someone committed to fostering a strong relationship with the children, let alone her boss. She also had the unforgivable sin of just not being very likable. It became a family joke—*after* she left my employ, I must point out—that whenever anything broke or went wrong the automatic response would be, "It's C~'s fault." Finally, in a moment of maturity, I called a halt to the joke.

The first lesson I learned was to focus on finding the right person for the job, and not worry about getting some long-term commitment. The second lesson was that none of them wanted to be paid on the books, and most considered it an inconvenience because they had to handle more paperwork. At the least they wanted to be paid the current market wage, which is an off-the-books determined wage, and then have the employer do the full mark-ups for employer and employee contributions, as well as deal with reams of paperwork that flowed in from different agencies in the state. Perhaps I'm wrong on this, as I didn't do a market analysis, but it was the only preference I ever saw. It was frustrating, but what followed was a train of wonderful young women: Gabrielle, who delivered a level of culinary excellence that added one more reason why the dinner hour was the best hour of the day; Kim, whose organizational skills had you thinking that she'd be running a company one day; and, of course, Christiani, the Austrian girl who looked to be straight out of *The Sound of Music* and had a wonderful laugh. They all did their duty, they all seemed to have fun, and I think the kids loved each one of them. They brought laughter and love to the house, and smoothed out many bumps in the road. A touch more discipline might have been a good idea, but that really wasn't their department.

They were so young, and they fit in so well, that it was almost like the kids had a much older sister, and one with a little authority. They were also quite pretty, a matter of true coincidence as they held no personal attraction for me, but perhaps if that middle-aged nanny had been a little friendlier. . . .

I tried to keep it simple for the kids. For a time I made a practice of leaving short notes for them at the breakfast table, reminding them of a music lesson or a dentist appointment or whatever. They would tell me they didn't need "the memos from Dad," but that was my insurance that they got the word. Their memories were not always up to speed early in the morning, nor was mine. I also wanted to give them some guidance on life, so I took a cue from the politicians and just recited my mantra: be good citizens in the home, study hard in school, grow up and find satisfying work, fill their own rice bowls, as the Chinese say, and have a big-screen TV in their home for when I would come to visit. They're working on the list.

When I think back on all the parenting years and try to put my finger on the greatest moments, it was when the children were filled with joy at what was going on in their young lives, and also when they were still south of the adolescent years. Once when I took Steven and a couple of his friends to a New Jersey Nets basketball game he paused halfway through his hot dog, turned to me and said, "Dad, this is the most fun there is." That kept me going for a long time. On another occasion, we were eating dinner and Amy told me that she and a few of her girl friends had started a club. She said they had named it "The Too Much Fun Club." Usually you wait till college for a club like that. The graduations and other special occasions were nice, but these little reflections that their lives were satisfying, that they had a structure in which a happy childhood could play out, were the best times. Perhaps, like the OSTAR, there will be no podium finish for me in the parenting game, but I can look in the mirror and know that I tried to be competitive, and I think I kept the big mistakes and wrong turns to a minimum. They say the passage through parenting never ends, but I'm no longer standing deck watches.

For me, the OSTAR has been my Too Much Fun Club, even if it has not always been the most fun there is.

The weather looks to continue fair, and I'm sure the sails have seen their last reefing hook for this passage. If the big genoa were still usable I would no doubt be holding a glass of something far weightier than the flavored water now keeping me hydrated. No matter, we'll be there soon and it's wonderful sailing in the light stuff.

A SURPRISE SQUALL

The two most powerful warriors are patience and time.

—LEO TOLSTOY

'm greatly enjoying the final watches. I have stood many watches at sea, some so beautiful that time evaporated, some so cold I was counting the minutes till they were over, some wet, some hot, and some tiresome, but all serious business. When you're standing watch on a crewed boat, the boat and the lives of the crew are in your hands. I'm often reminded of one of the "permanent general orders" I learned in the Marine Corps, the one that required you "to quit your post only when properly relieved." One of the great things about crewed sailing is that a formal watch schedule is maintained and everyone can enjoy some down time when they're off watch.

In solo sailing, the watch schedule is out the window. Every time you step on deck to look around or check the trim of the sails you're on watch, but you can't be on watch 24/7, so you pick your spots and take your chances. Radar and ship alarms are your electronic assistants, as well as a certain vigilance that stays with you even in the bunk where your ears are the primary alarm sensors, but in the end, you quit your post when you damn well feel like it and are comfortable with the risks.

These shallower coastal waters seem friendlier than the more rural ocean neighborhoods, and their color palettes lean more toward the pastels, but I do not consider them benign. In fact, strong winds can turn shallow waters violent more quickly than in the open ocean, where the surface has the steadying effect of two thousand fathoms of water. I'm starting to feel comfortable with most of what the ocean can throw at me, at least this ocean in this season, but there are no big winds in store for us as we make our way home.

We're in barely enough breeze to maintain headway and I have plenty of time to observe the approach of the Coast Guard cutter, a brilliant white against the deep blues of today's sky and sea, and the red blaze of the USCG insignia showing proud. The expected radio call soon arrives, and after the usual formalities I'm asked when I plan to arrive in Newport, to which I respond, "As soon as possible." It is good to be talking to someone other than myself, and I have a fine chat with the young and serious voice from the lovely cutter. I feel mildly embarrassed to be sitting here waiting for wind when almost everyone has arrived, but after the feeling rattles around for a bit I let it go.

The Coast Guard men and women, Coasties as sailors respectfully call them, are an impressive crew. Their official motto, *Semper paratus* (always ready), is similar to the Marines' *Semper fidelis* (always faithful). They're heavily burdened these days, not least by their roles in maritime policing, but I think their hearts are always drawn to the search and rescue function; or perhaps that is just something I want to believe as a sailor. The Coast Guard used to have a saying: "You have to go out, but you don't have to come back." That reflected their ethic that you always go out to assist a distressed mariner regardless of the conditions. Rather like the Marines' saying, "Leave no one behind on the battlefield." I've been told that the Coast Guard has tried to change the mind-set to one dictating, "You don't have to go out, but if you go, you do have to come back." A rational mind would applaud this change. Some mariners find themselves in distress due to their own stupidity, and then want to be saved at immense danger to others and under horrific conditions. Should the government risk the lives of its people, not to mention the cost of the helicopters, on missions that lack a high probability of success? The Coasties are young and brave, and they will always want to go. Management, their high command, has to use prudence and restraint. Yes, a rational mind would applaud this latest dilution in the warrior culture.

I'm chomping on dried fruit as the day winds down. In the absence of any remaining sweets or treats this is the closest thing left. If the breeze holds I will be in port by breakfast. I pop Dylan's *Blood on the Tracks* CD in the stereo and enjoy an evening on deck, the darkness held at bay by the stars, steering through the night with the Big Dipper high over my shoulder.

Suddenly the wind is up and blowing, the visit of an unnoticed squall. A second surprise quickly follows. The sheet controlling the headsail has slipped off the winch. Obviously the captain of this vessel neglected to lock the sheet in properly. Pure carelessness! The long line is quickly trailing in the water, leaving the unleashed sail flopping crazily in the wind. With the working sheet temporarily sidelined, I quickly tack *Rubicon* through the wind to put the lazy sheet on the other side of the boat to work holding the now wind-filled sail. Once more I snap on my harness and make my way forward, this time to retrieve the errant sheet as *Rubicon* rockets along. Lying on the side deck, I reach out and finally manage to grab the wet and slippery line. I then haul it onto the boat and lead it back to the cockpit where it can return to its winch, and we can return to the proper tack.

The squall should have been a nonevent, not another reminder of how quickly life on a sailboat can change, but I had been complacent, sitting on the helm seat, dreamily listening to a Dylan ballad, enjoying the beautiful endgame of this passage, and contemplating my evening off the boat. Of course I hadn't left the boat, but a few hours earlier I had used the sat phone to call Barbara. She was already in Newport, ensconced in a local restaurant eating dinner with friends. The phone had been passed around and I felt warmed by the short conversations and warm wishes. I was ready to join the scene. Desires flooded back: a fresh shirt, a glass of wine, an embrace, conversation, fresh vegetables, perhaps a steak. I heard myself mumble, "It sure was nice getting off the boat this evening." That's when the squall hit. What happened to those reminders about vigilance that I kept telling myself? I've been given a slap in the face and that's a good thing. I really don't want to get off the boat when I'm still 50 miles offshore.

THE FOG BREAKS

Among the most useful and excellent arts,
navigation has always taken first place.

—SAMUEL DE CHAMPLAIN

There was no sleep on my last night at sea. We're closing on the coast and I need to be aware of any traffic and steer a true course. But the night was also beautiful. Aside from the cluster-fumble of last evening, it was a gift of a sail—just cool enough to require a sweatshirt, stars lighting the path, and a fresh but undemanding breeze. I would glance down at the compass periodically, but mainly I just kept our orientation to the Big Dipper as we rolled along. I had every expectation that I would be enjoying an egg-laden breakfast ashore, catching up with Barbara, and downing multiple refills of steaming coffee, but just as the dawn was breaking, and approximately 15 nautical miles from the finish, the wind dropped to a zephyr and breakfast was a can of peaches and some crackers.

This final day of the OSTAR is proving a lot more difficult than I expected. The fog rolled in as the wind dissipated, and right now there is just enough of a breeze to keep us sailing. I'm watching my navigation carefully, as well as the radar, which fortunately escaped the equipment carnage of the passage. These are my home waters, but I've never come in with heavy fog and no chartplotter after a night without sleep. The radio has suddenly come alive with a constant hum of activity. The approaches to Narragansett Bay see the transit of everything from large ships and commercial fishing boats, to sailboats and the smallest runabouts. The morning is spent peering through the fog and keeping an ear out for any engine noise coming across the waters.

I have retrieved the U.S. flag from its locker and set the pole in its stern bracket. I flew the flag on the start day and felt proud as we crossed the line with the stars and stripes flying, but by day two the fleet was dispersed, so I rolled it up for the passage.

It occurs to me that even though there is no GPS feed to the chartplotter, I can still power up the unit and scroll to the correct chart on the plotter. With this done, I use my handheld GPS unit to get a position, and then place the cursor on the screen in our position on the chart. Seeing the visual improves my spirits immediately, and I'm updating the position every 15 minutes. I had been doing this with the paper chart since first light, but with my hands rather full steering the boat and keeping a lookout, this is a more workable arrangement.

The approach to Newport is not a difficult one, but you can't wander too far from your course. There are reefs, which have sunk more than a few boats at the end of their transatlantic journeys, and I want to be on the proper side of them today. When I try to radio to the committee boat, I discover that the contacts on the remote microphone used at the helm have corroded and it is no longer functioning, so my final hour of the race is spent juggling the portable VHF radio, the handheld GPS, and the wheel as we drive to the finish. Sailing is filled with juggling acts.

It turns out that the fog is an offshore phenomenon, and as I get to within a half mile of the finish line off Castle Hill, the fog ends and I sail into a beautiful sunny afternoon. Two boats are waiting to record my crossing. It feels like a movie. *Rubicon* ghosts over the finish line to OSTAR 2009, the end of a 39-day and 7-hour passage. The light-air finish is the perfect bookend to the limp breeze at the start, but we were certainly visited by many and interesting winds along the way. Barbara and friends are taking pictures from the reception boat. The elation of the finish burns away my fatigue. As my daughter might say, it was so worth it.

Rubicon approaching the finish line.

There will be no hint in the pictures of the difficulties on this final day, or those of the thirty-nine previous ones, but it has been, at times, a tricky affair. Sleep-deprived and cloaked in fog, I had entertained the absurd thought of quitting the race only miles from the finish line and requesting an early tow. I splashed my face with plenty of fresh water, which was no longer a rationed commodity, and cleansed myself of that nutty idea.

The race committee boat is joined by a towboat from the yacht club. Friends clamber aboard, and Barbara and I embrace while Kevin takes charge of dropping the sails and securing the towline. *Rubicon* is towed the few hundred yards to the dock. All along the harbor people on the moored boats are cheering and blowing their boat horns, and somewhere a cannon fires. It is my good luck to arrive on Friday, July 3, just as Newport is getting set for the July 4 weekend, but it is very touching to receive such a welcome, particularly as I know that I am the second to last boat in. Norm Bailey, the commodore of the Newport Yacht Club and a great supporter of the race, tells me that all of the finishers received similar receptions, though the middle-of-night arrivals were quieter. The crowd doesn't seem to care about my position in the contest, and right now neither do I.

The author crossing the finishing line, after forty days alone at sea.

The obligatory meeting with U.S. Customs is quickly over when a friendly official checks my passport, takes an admiring look over *Rubicon*, and congratulates me on the passage. Repairing to the Newport Yacht Club, drinks magically appear before me, and Norm presents me with the City of Newport Medal and my OSTAR plaque. Both items are received by all the finishers, and they will be treasured mementos of the saga. The round of applause from the sailors in the club is as delicious as the cold beer.

There is an old Turkish expression, "May it be behind you"— which I jotted down from Paul Theroux's book, *The Pillars of Hercules*—and now, on the fortieth day, it is indeed behind me. I feel a certain pride. The passage has been made under sail, and *Rubicon* has crossed the finish line two days before the deadline. Mixed with the pride are relief, joy, and gratitude. The effect of this emotional cocktail, combined with a fair level of fatigue, is mildly intoxicating and very pleasurable. It is good to be back on land, to be back with people and back on the calendar, and it is good to be home.

EPILOGUE

As I look back on my OSTAR race, many questions are fired at the press conference in my mind.

What do you have to say to your fellow OSTAR sailors?

I say "bravo" to all who made the attempt, "well done" to all the finishers, and "outstanding" to the class winners. To JanKees Lampe, the Dutch entrepreneur who rocketed his Open 40 race boat to achieve line honors as the first to finish, and to Will Sayer, a friendly and unassuming Briton who became the overall winner on corrected time in a stout cruising boat, I say "inspirational!"

Are you satisfied with how you did in the race?

The short answer is no. Thirty-one boats started the race, six turned back, one was lost, and twenty-four crossed the finish line. I was number twenty-three.

Do you have any regrets?

Yes, I regret that I didn't sail the boat faster, and when all the nattering about equipment problems is over, that's the bottom line.

Does your performance in the race really matter to you?

Yes, and perhaps more than it should. I believe I gave it my best shot. Now I know how I could have given it a much better shot. That's called experience.

Was it the transformative experience that you suspected it might be when you untied the dock lines in Plymouth?

Yes, I think so, and the thought occurs that it might not have been if the race had been a smooth sail, assuming it is possible for any solo transit of the North Atlantic to qualify as smooth.

It may be too soon to say that my OSTAR was transformative. Actions flow from true transformations, so perhaps the jury is still out on mine, but I feel that some rewiring has been effected. The connections between my heart, brain, and soul have been tuned, and my new synthesis is a return to the basics, to my three Rs of life: risks, relationships, and roles. If these can be managed, most of the other stuff will fall into place or not be worth worrying about.

As Aleksandr Solzhenitsyn asked in his classic *In the First Circle*, "If one is forever cautious, can one remain a human being?" The question is spiritual, and the answer is no. I advised my children many times to stop and think before taking a risk; stupid risks are just that. But if memory serves, I cautioned them almost as frequently about the foolishness of timidity. As Erica Jong said, "The trouble is, if you don't risk anything, you risk even more." Sorting out the risks, and digging deep to face the worthy ones, are the challenges that define a life.

My friend Mark once relayed to me his father's admonition about how to build a life, saying, "When it's time to go to work, you have to really want to go to work, and when it's time to go home, you must really want to go home." I smiled when I first heard that line, as one does when hearing words passed down that seem too basic for quotation marks. But I came to realize that it tells a great deal of what you need to know for a meaningful life.

The old answers I once had to the existential question have dissolved over the years. I did not expect to find replacements, or learn the true meaning of life, in the middle of the ocean, any more than I would have expected to find it at the top of a mountain, but surprisingly I think I have, at least a meaning that will suffice for me. My high school chemistry teacher—Mr. Leinkraus—had already revealed it to me over forty years ago when he said, "Be a professional at what you're doing." I wrote it down when I was sixteen, but I kept looking for more. There isn't much more, just that, and of course love, and the Golden Rule.

So take the right risks, preserve the right relationships, and play your roles well. Mine have been as son, sibling, soldier, student, worker, husband, father, partner, friend, and sailor. Being retired is not a role any more than cashing a paycheck is a role, but there are scripts out there and more roles to find. Directors sometimes tell actors, "You are more likely to act yourself into feeling than feel yourself into action. So act! Whatever it is you know you should do, do it."

The final question in my mental news conference arrives:

What can you learn from sailing?

I don't know the full answer. What I do know is that sailing is about more than the ability to tie the right knot, choose the optimal sail combination, or develop a keen weather eye—it is about introducing ourselves to the 70-plus percent of our planet that is not terra firma, an introduction that inevitably leads to a more intimate knowledge of ourselves, and that is the ultimate reward and the true comfort of a passage under sail.

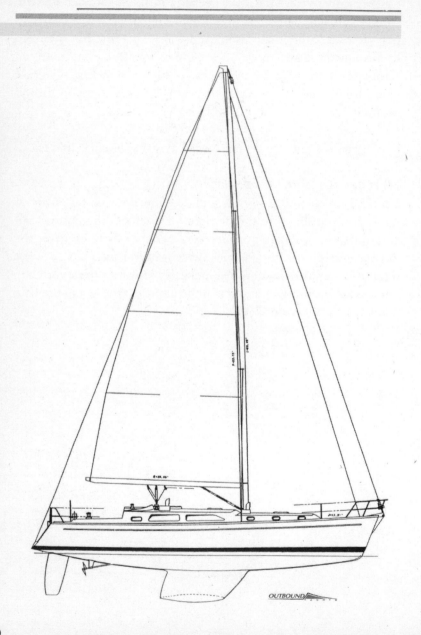

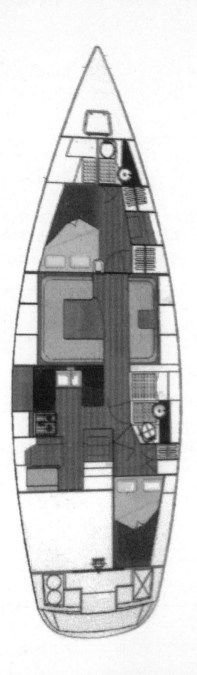

ROYAL WESTERN SINGLEHANDED TRANSATLANTIC RACE
2009—The Thirteenth OSTAR

Plymouth–Newport
25-May-09
Started: 31
Finished: 24

CLASSES
Pen Duick–IRC 1   Eira–IRC 3
Gipsy Moth–IRC 1   Manureva–Open 50
Jester–IRC 2   Three Cheers–MOCRA 1

Skipper	Yacht	LOA	Class	Elapsed / Corrected Time	O/A Place	Class Place	Corr. Place	Nation
LAMPE, JanKees	LA PROMESSE	40	PD	17 17 40 / 21 15 18	1	1	3	NED
CRAIGIE, Rob	JBELLINO	40	PD	19 00 10 / 20 13 34	2	2	1	GBR
WESTERMAN, Roberto	SPINNING WHEEL	40	PD	19 03 14 / 23 09 10	3	3	4	ITA
WHITE, Hannah	PURE SOLO	40	PD	20 00 22 / 21 15 16	4	4	2	GBR
HURLEY, Barry	DINAH	35	GM	20 22 35 / 21 06 37	5	1	1	IRL
ZOCCOLI, Luca	IN DIREZIONE OSTINATA E CONTRARIA	35	PD	20 22 39 / 26 11 51	6	5	7	ITA
FREEMAN, Jerry	QII	35	PD	21 02 49 / 23 16 08	7	6	5	GBR
MEAD, Oscar	KING OF SHAVES	34	GM	21 12 24 / 21 18 36	8	2	2	GBR
MILLER, Katie	BLUQUBE	33	PD	21 18 53 / 23 18 59	9	7	6	GBR

Skipper	Yacht	LOA	Class	Elapsed / Corrected Time	O/A Place	Class Place	Corr. Place	Nation
ROTTGERING, Uwe	FANFAN!	40	GM	21 22 42 / 22 06 36	10	3	3	GER
NANNINI, Marco	BRITISH BEAGLE	36	J	21 23 44 / 20 16 04	11	1	1	ITA
SWETS, Huib	VIJAYA	42	GM	22 03 41 / 22 10 35	12	4	4	NED
KOOPMANS, Dick	JAGER	35	J	22 04 35 / 21 21 39	13	2	3	NED
BOOSMAN, Bart	DE FRANSCHMAN	30	J	22 21 04 / 21 18 09	14	3	2	NED
SAYER, Will	ELMARLEEN	32	E	23 01 30 / 19 22 46	15	1	1	GBR
HILDESLEY, Pip	CAZENOVE CAPITAL	39	GM	23 14 05 / 23 14 38	16	5	5	GBR
CHALANDRE, Christian	OLBIA	33	E	24 09 06 / 21 21 25	17	2	2	FRA
FALLA, John	BANJAARD	37	J	24 20 55 / 23 22 49	18	5	4	GBR
COLLINS, Michael	FLAMINGO LADY	33	E	27 05 31 / 24 10 51	19	3	3	GBR
PETTY, Andrew	JEMIMA NICHOLAS	40	J	28 15 57 / 27 13 48	20	6	6	GBR
CROWTHER, Peter	SUOMI KUDU	38	J	29 02 15 / 27 07 39	21	7	5	GBR
BOURKE, Peter	RUBICON	45	GM	39 07 56 / 41 00 31	22	6	6	USA
ALCORN, Geoff	WIND OF LORNE II	36	E	43 07 55 / Over time limit				GBR
WHEATLEY, Mervyn	TAMARIND	42	J	22 05 47 / Retired				GBR
BOUCHACOURT, Jacques	OKAMI	50	PD	Retired				FRA
CUMMING, Rob	EGOTRIPP	40	PD	Power failure				GBR
TORTOLANI, Gianfranco	CITTÀ DI SALERNO	30	PD	Capsized, rescued by ship				ITA
BRANT, Paul	NINJOD	35	GM	Cracked bulkhead and other problems				GBR
SNODGRASS, Jonathan	LEXIA	32	E	Retired				GBR

Skipper	Yacht	LOA	Class	Elapsed / Corrected Time	O/A Place	Class Place	Corr. Place	Nation
CASENEUVE, Anne	CROISIÈRES ANNE CASENEUVE	40	TC	Broken rudder				FRA
GELDER, Reini	LIGHT FOR THE WORLD	40	TC	Rigging failure				AUT

(Courtesy the Royal Western Yacht Club of England)

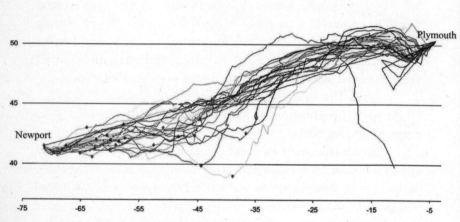

Data plot of the course sailed by the thirty-one boats that started the 2009 OSTAR. As with any race, the course variation is as varied as the winds and boats. *(Courtesy the Royal Western Yacht Club of England)*

ACKNOWLEDGMENTS

Whatever growth I have experienced as a writer has received direction and momentum from the keen insights of: Nancy Aronie, Jim Bartlett, Elisabeth Broggi, Dinah Lenny, Donna Moreau, and Grace Talusan. They have my deep appreciation, as well as my personal assurance that I will never write another memoir.

I extend my appreciation to Another Sundown Publishing Company for permission to quote the Kate Wolf lyrics used as an epigraph in Day 33.

I particularly want to thank the early readers of *Sea Trials* for taking the time from other pursuits, and for their thoughtful comments. So, to: Margaret, David, Paul, Kevin, Tommy, Hank, Huw, and Barbara, thank you!

Turning to the crucial ingredient, I gratefully acknowledge Molly Mulhern of McGraw-Hill Education/International Marine, first for believing in my manuscript, and then for bringing her wisdom and experience to bear in turning it into a book.

Finally, I give my thanks to the United States Marine Corps. I'm glad that we separated honorably over forty years ago, but I know that without their lessons this would have been a different book, assuming I'd been around to write it. Therefore, all author royalties have been assigned to The Semper Fi Fund, a wonderful organization that serves wounded veterans from all branches of the military, and their families.

ABOUT THE AUTHOR

Peter J. Bourke was born in London, and came to the United States at age 6 when his family emigrated from the United Kingdom. Following three years in the Marine Corps, Bourke went to college on the GI Bill and discovered economics. This is his first book. Peter lives in Newport, Rhode Island.